Fullerism as Opposed to Calvinism

Fullerism as Opposed to Calvinism

A Historical and Theological Comparison of the Missiology of Andrew Fuller and John Calvin

A. CHADWICK MAULDIN

WIPF & STOCK · Eugene, Oregon

FULLERISM AS OPPOSED TO CALVINISM
A Historical and Theological Comparison of the Missiology
of Andrew Fuller and John Calvin

Copyright © 2011 A. Chadwick Mauldin. All rights reserved. Except for brief quotations in critical publications or reviews, no part of this book may be reproduced in any manner without prior written permission from the publisher. Write: Permissions, Wipf and Stock Publishers, 199 W. 8th Ave., Suite 3, Eugene, OR 97401.

Wipf & Stock
An Imprint of Wipf and Stock Publishers
199 W. 8th Ave., Suite 3
Eugene, OR 97401
www.wipfandstock.com

ISBN 13: 978-1-60899-832-6

Manufactured in the U.S.A.

All scripture quotations, unless otherwise indicated, are taken from the Holy Bible, New International Version®, NIV®. Copyright ©1973, 1978, 1984 by Biblica, Inc.™ Used by permission of Zondervan. All rights reserved worldwide.

*To April Ann Mauldin, beloved wife and friend,
whose enduring love and support helped make this project possible.*

Contents

Foreword by Michael A. G. Haykin   ix
Preface   xi
Acknowledgements   xiii

1   **Preliminary Issues   1**
    Trends in Baptist Theology
    A Call for Baptist Distinctives
    Fullerism as opposed to Calvinism: The Thesis

2   **Historical Survey   13**
    The Particular Baptists
    Particular Baptist Influences
    Andrew Fuller

3   **Doctrinal Study of John Calvin   29**
    Biographical Data
    Prevailing Sentiments on the Reformers and Missions
    Calvin's Role in Missions
    Missiological Critiques

4   **Doctrinal Study of Andrew Fuller   49**
    Fuller and the BMS
    Fuller and *The Gospel Worthy of All Acceptation*
    Missiological Principles

5   **Conclusion   66**
    Summary
    Points of Agreement
    Points of Disagreement
    Concluding Remarks

Appendix A: An Interview with Dr. James Leo Garrett, Jr.   73
Appendix B: A Selection of Andrew Fuller's Letters   85
Bibliography   109
Index: Name and Subject   113

Foreword

Reading about Andrew Fuller

MICHAEL A. G. HAYKIN

Having picked up this new book on the eighteenth-century Baptist theologian Andrew Fuller, you might be asking yourself, "What is so significant about this self-taught divine?" Well, for starters, in the entire history of the English Baptists, there are only two or three other authors that equal him in theological impact and importance. In the previous century, two London pastors, Benjamin Keach (1640–1704) and John Gill (1697–1771), were the two major theologians that helped express and define the Baptist vision. People today often think of John Bunyan (1628–88) as a key figure in this community. Bunyan, however, was committed to open communion and open membership, while the vast majority of his co-religionists were closed communion and closed membership, and this meant that his role among his contemporary English Baptists was quite diminished. It was only in the late Georgian era and then in the Victorian period, that most of his works became popular. And after Fuller, the only figure that comes to mind is Charles Haddon Spurgeon (1834–92), whose theological influence was enormous but who really cannot be considered a systematic theologian like Gill or Fuller. It is noteworthy that Spurgeon once described Fuller as "the greatest theologian" of his century. And it bears remembering that Fuller's influence was also deeply felt across the Atlantic, where those indebted to his thought became known as "Fullerites." Southern Baptist historian A. H. Newman once said that "his influence on American Baptists" was "incalculable."

Fuller's first major work, *The Gospel Worthy of All Acceptation*, which appeared in 1785 with a second edition in 1801, proved to be an epoch-making book that decisively refuted the hyper-Calvinism that gripped many sectors of the Baptist denomination in England and Wales and laid the theological foundations for the modern missionary movement. In 1793 he issued an extensive refutation of Socinianism or Unitarianism, *The Calvinistic and Socinian Systems examined and Compared, as to their Moral Tendency*, which well displays the Christ-centered nature of eighteenth-century Evangelical thought. Fuller also penned the key Baptist rebuttals of Deism and Sandemanianism, the latter an eighteenth-century form of "easy-believism." Along with these major volumes there was a steady stream of smaller tracts and treatises, published sermons, association letters, journal articles, and occasional pieces that expressed Fuller's vision of what it means to be a Baptist.

Thankfully the last few years have seen a revival of interest in Fuller's thought, of which this book by Chad Mauldin is in part the product. Mauldin tackles a big question of reception history, namely, given that Fuller identified himself as a Calvinist, what exactly are the details of Fuller's embrace of Calvinism? Where does he agree and where does he disagree with the great French Reformer? This question has been asked before, notably by A. H. Kirkby and E. F. Clipsham in the 1950s and 1960s, but, in light of the renaissance of interest in the work of Fuller, it bears new investigation, and this new study by Mauldin is an excellent starting-place for rethinking this issue. Not all will agree with his conclusions, but it is absolutely vital to think through his argument, for both reasons of academic scholarship and contemporary Baptist life.

Michael A. G. Haykin
Dundas, Ontario, Canada
June 1, 2010.

Preface

This book is a historical and theological comparison of Andrew Fuller and John Calvin. Essentially, this study is questioning whether Fullerism, for the Baptist, is a more appropriate theological descriptor than Calvinism as it respects, primarily, missiological concerns. Chapter 1 progresses this task by analyzing the influence of Calvinistic doctrine within modern Baptist life. Also, this survey of Calvinistic influence is combined with a consideration of certain historic Baptist distinctives.

As a means of establishing historical context, chapter 2 provides a discussion of the origins of the seventeenth-century English Particular Baptists. In addition, as a descendent of the English Particular Baptists and a primary subject of this book, this chapter presents a biographical account of Andrew Fuller.

Chapter 3 is an analysis of Calvin's missiology. This examination is accomplished by, first, discussing Calvin's biographical data. Also, a description of Calvin's missiology is developed through an interaction with his writings and through the witness of history. Finally, this chapter provides a critique of two missiological characteristics related to Calvin's thought.

Andrew Fuller is the subject of chapter 4. This chapter examines Fuller's role in the missions revival of eighteenth-century English Baptist life. Also, a detailing of Fuller's missiological convictions and thought is presented in order to develop a discernable missiology.

Chapter 5 concludes by performing several tasks. First, it provides a brief summary of this book's major arguments—offered for the sake of clarity. Second, this chapter highlights those areas within Calvin and Fuller's missiology where there is agreement and disagreement. Finally, as a result of the evidence presented, the research question of this book is answered.

Acknowledgments

The completion of a project such as this is rarely conducted within a vacuum. Rather, such a task is often the result of hard work within the context of God's grace, much support, and disciplined expert advice. This book (which was originally my MATh thesis at Southwestern Baptist Theological Seminary—slightly revised and expanded) is no exception.

I would like to extend a sincere gesture of gratitude to Dr. Malcolm B. Yarnell III whose involvement with this project has proven invaluable. Dr. Yarnell's advice and insistence upon objectivity has undoubtedly impacted my perspective and, consequently, the quality of this book. Likewise, Dr. Paige Patterson is truly appreciated for his ardent commitment to intellectual honesty and integrity. He has without question helped to shape the content of this book and my development as a scholar. Both of these men truly stand in the noble tradition that has long been established by Southwestern Baptist Theological Seminary.

Also, much gratitude is due to Dr. Michael A. G. Haykin. Dr. Haykin has provided several challenging comments and suggestions pertaining to this project that have proven quite helpful. Dr. Haykin's willingness to readily share his wealth of knowledge is a testament to his character as a Christian scholar. I do, however, in light of the persons just thanked, take full responsibility for the content of this book. Any inadvertent mistakes found within are certainly to be thought of as mine alone.

In addition, Dr. Haykin is warmly thanked for his kindness in making available a copy of a collection of Andrew Fuller's unpublished letters, the originals of which are housed at Regent's Park College, Oxford University, Oxford. Angus Library (at Regent's Park College, Oxford) must surely be thanked as well for their permission, allowing me to transcribe and include in this book several of Fuller's letters (most of which were unpublished).

Additionally, a debt of gratitude is due to Happy Hill Farm Academy along with the Shipman family. For the last eight years I have been employed by this organization, and the kindness and support from the Shipman family throughout my undergraduate and graduate studies are acknowledged and greatly appreciated.

Finally, my pursuit in answering God's call for theological study would have been utterly impossible had it not been for a godly and devout wife. April Ann Mauldin has been and continues to be a source of inspiration and encouragement. Further, the support and understanding of my beloved children (Clayton, Jackson, and Carly) have been a constant reminder of God's grace. I would also be remiss if an expression of gratitude were not extended to the following immediate family members: Art and Jackie Mauldin (parents), Betty Lewis (grandmother), Lank and Liz Easterling (in-laws), and Sue Ann Easterling (dearly departed mother in-law). Their enduring encouragement and support have been greatly appreciated.

A. Chadwick Mauldin
Granbury, Texas
July 2010

1

Preliminary Issues

HISTORICALLY MANY BAPTISTS HAVE clearly been willing to associate themselves, theologically, with Calvinism.[1] This is largely based upon the fact that a number of Baptists throughout history have been committed to a Calvinistic soteriology. It is unfortunate, however, that this Calvinistic association among modern Baptists, in its practical expressions, often fails to consider the broader body of Reformed doctrine such as missiology and ecclesiology, in addition to soteriology.[2] A deeper study of these Reformed issues would be prudent in order to determine whether theological conflicts of interest or, perhaps, certain incompatibilities are present within Reformed theology when compared to Baptist doctrine.

Richard A. Muller makes an interesting argument against the notion of a "five point" Calvinist.[3] He recounts a conversation with a Baptist minister who considered himself to be an adherent to all "five points" of Calvinism. Muller is suspicious of this common theological descriptor. He insists that Reformed doctrine is necessarily much broader than one might presume if one is holding only to the "five points" outside of the proper context. In other words, the "five points" were an occasional construction in response to the Remonstrant controversy (1610), and they

---

1. For the purpose of this paper, "Calvinist" and "Reformed" will be used interchangeably.

2. Reformed Baptist churches often celebrate Presbyterian or other Reformed writings (and in many cases rightly so) without an appropriate tentativeness with respect to the implications or assertions of these writings regarding ecclesiology and missiology.

3. "Five point" Calvinism is, of course, referring to the common soteriological doctrines of total depravity, unconditional election, limited atonement, irresistible grace, and perseverance of the saints.

can only be properly understood in the complete context of Reformed confessional heritage.[4]

Muller maintains that the Calvinist must necessarily align himself or herself with the Reformed confessions by affirming infant baptism, the sacraments as a means of grace, the notion of a visible and invisible church, and amillennialism. Reformed theology, says Muller, is a carefully biblically reasoned and systematically articulated entity of which the "five points" are only one feature.[5] Muller, it seems then, considers an important portion of Baptist distinctives incompatible with Calvinistic soteriology.

This book does not intend to argue, with Muller, that Calvinistic soteriology is necessarily unacceptable or incompatible for the Baptist. In fact, Baptists have a long and rich association with Reformed soteriological convictions (a treatment of this association will be considered later). Instead, this writer is questioning the suitability of Calvinism as a Baptist nomenclature or theological landmark. Muller is right, at least in part: Calvinism is, of course, much more comprehensive than the doctrine of salvation. Baptist identity and convictions must be, likewise, concerned with the full spectrum of Christian doctrine and practice.

TRENDS IN BAPTIST THEOLOGY

One might question the relevancy of a discussion over Calvinism as a suitable theological descriptor for the Baptist. In other words, is there a significant presence of Calvinism within current Baptist life? If modern Baptist scholarship is any indication, then the answer to this question must be in the affirmative. Perhaps a brief overview of several Calvinistic or Reformed leaning Baptist theologians would prove helpful in illustrating this current trend. This section, then, will focus on a representative group of academic theologians who are making notable contributions to Baptist scholarship.[6]

---

4. Muller, "How Many Points," 425–26.
5. Muller, "How Many Points," 427, 433.
6. The individuals covered here are only representative. There are many other notable contemporary Baptist theologians who are associated with a Calvinistic soteriology such as: Timothy George, Mark Dever, Al Mohler, and Michael Haykin among others.

Wayne Grudem

Wayne Grudem (1948–) is a prominent systematic theologian whose work is widely appreciated and much discussed today. Grudem's education (theological and otherwise) was carried out at Harvard (B.A., 1970), Westminster Theological Seminary, (M.Div., 1973), and Cambridge (Ph.D., 1979). His most significant work, perhaps, is his one volume systematic theology entitled: *Systematic Theology: An Introduction to Biblical Doctrine*. Although Grudem has been a part of other denominational movements (Bible and Vineyard congregations), he is ordained as a Baptist minister (1974).[7]

In his systematic theology, Grudem seems to affirm all five points of Dortian Calvinism. For example, in chapter 24, while avoiding the term total depravity, Grudem promotes the doctrine by claiming that lost humanity totally lacks spiritual good. He makes sure to avoid the misunderstanding that mankind is incapable of any good at all. Rather, Grudem intends to convey that there is no part of humanity unaffected by sin. Even the good that one may contribute to society is touched in some way by sin or depravity. Consequently, Grudem concludes, mankind cannot, apart from Christ, be in right relationship with God.[8]

The doctrine of unconditional election is also affirmed by Grudem. In his chapter on election and reprobation, Grudem argues that election can only be unconditional. He concludes this after having rejected the popular notion that God's election is based simply on his foreknowledge. Grudem acknowledges that many look to Romans 8:28 as support for the idea that foreknowledge is the key to understanding God's election. He responds, however, by arguing that Paul is not communicating God's foreknowledge of facts about people (the fact that they will respond to the gospel). Instead, Paul is speaking of God's intimate knowledge of his redeemed children. God foreknows those persons whom he will redeem. As a result, Grudem promotes election as unconditional, unprompted by human activity.[9]

Limited atonement can be perceived as well—Grudem refers to it as particular atonement—in chapter 27 of his theology. Grudem accepts the truthfulness of the saying, "Christ died for his people only," when

---

7. Garrett, *Baptist Theology*, 683–84.
8. Grudem, *Systematic Theology*, 497.
9. Grudem, *Systematic Theology*, 676–79.

addressing the extent of the atonement. He is quick, however, to reject any notion of particular atonement being an impediment to the free proclamation of the gospel. In fact, Grudem believes that an affirmation of particular atonement is in no way in conflict with the conviction that Christ's death brings the gospel call to all persons. While maintaining that particular atonement should be affirmed because of its logical uniformity (in the context of Reformed soteriology), Grudem admits that there is no direct biblical witness of the doctrine of limited atonement. As a result, limited atonement or particular atonement is cautiously affirmed by Grudem.[10]

Grudem's chapter on regeneration reveals his alignment with the doctrine of irresistible grace. According to Grudem, God's regeneration and effectual calling of a person (regeneration precedes faith) ensures the certainty of saving faith. In this way, grace is understood as irresistible. It is God's loving work in the heart of mankind that brings about a saving response. This work of God is necessary for the facilitating of humanity's voluntary response to God in faith.[11] Apparently, Grudem affirms the Calvinistic doctrine of irresistible grace.[12]

Finally, Grudem is committed to Reformed soteriology in the sense that he upholds the doctrine of perseverance of the saints. Grudem maintains that all truly regenerate persons endure to the end. Here Grudem stresses God's care for his children in ensuring that they will not be lost; they will have eternal life (John 6:38–40). There is an emphasis, however, of the individual's biblical call for perseverance. Grudem takes seriously the many warning passages issued by the biblical writers. These passages, according to Grudem, are not in conflict with the doctrine of perseverance. Instead, he concludes that those who fall away possess only external indications of salvation and, therefore, are not truly regenerate.[13]

---

10. Grudem, *Systematic Theology*, 601–03.

11. Grudem is presumably referring to some sort of compatibilistic idea of free will; however, he does not attempt to support or detail this idea within the scope of a philosophical structure. Rather, he is satisfied to appeal only to scriptures affirming both God's sovereignty and man's moral agency. Grudem, *Systematic Theology*, 320.

12. Grudem, *Systematic Theology*, 700.

13. Grudem, *Systematic Theology*, 788–94.

Thomas J. Nettles

Thomas Nettles (1946—) is a noted historian who is currently a professor of historical theology at The Southern Baptist Theological Seminary. Nettles grew up in Brandon, Mississippi and graduated from college in that state from Mississippi College (B.A., 1968). He continued his education at Southwestern Baptist Theological Seminary, completing two degrees (B.D., 1971; Ph.D., 1976).[14] Southwestern Seminary was Nettles's first teaching post beginning in 1976. While at Southwestern, Nettles, along with L. Russ Bush, made a needed and notable contribution to Southern Baptist life and theology with the book entitled, *Baptists and the Bible* (Moody Press, 1980). This work addressed the turmoil in Southern Baptist life at that time as it related to scriptural authority and inerrancy. Essentially, Bush and Nettles argued that Baptists throughout history have uniformly insisted upon biblical inerrancy.[15]

In his book *By His Grace and for His Glory*, Nettles operates on the presumption that Calvinistic soteriology is true and makes the argument that Dortian Calvinism was the touchstone for Baptist theology until the era of E. Y. Mullins (early twentieth century). To Nettles, the "doctrines of grace" are foundational for true assurance of salvation, liberty of conscience, and a right understanding and practice of missions. Further, Nettles claims that "the purest biblical presentation of the gospel glides upon the waters of the Doctrines of Grace."[16]

He outlines the Calvinism of such Baptist figures as Benjamin Keach, John Bunyan, John Gill, and Andrew Fuller among others.[17] Nettles also concludes that it is E. Y. Mullins who began, through his theological method, the shift away from the "doctrines of grace" in Baptist life. Notice the lament as Nettles describes the theological contribution of Mullins:

> Although the doctrine of unconditional election was accepted by E. Y. Mullins, both his theological method and his specific exposition of divine election served to compromise the earlier views of Dagg, Boyce, Broadus, Manly, Mell and others. Emphasis on human consciousness and experience so predominate in the

---

14. Garrett, *Baptist Theology*, 666.
15. For further details, see Duesing, "Luther Russell Bush III," 9–10.
16. Nettles, *By His Grace and for His Glory*, 27, 351, 368, 383.
17. Nettles, *By His Grace and for His Glory*, 55–130.

totality of Mullins's theology that human decision and freedom eventually overshadow and crowd out effectual divine activity.[18]

In the second part of his book, Nettles moves away from historical accounts of Calvinism and provides the reader with a theological exposition of Calvinistic soteriology. He describes unconditional election as God's choosing certain persons to be saved before the foundation of the world. He presents this doctrine as one of the most feared and neglected teachings among modern evangelicals and posits that unconditional election is the basis "for every legitimate enterprise of Christian endeavor."[19]

Next, Nettles treats depravity and effectual calling (irresistible grace) together in the same section. He argues that these two doctrines are so connected that separate treatments are not warranted. For example, mankind is without the ability to repent when confronted with the gospel as a result of total depravity. This condition leaves the individual in absolute need of God's undeserved gift of irresistible grace. God's free and uncaused gift is mankind's only hope of salvation.[20]

Nettles moves on to address the doctrine of limited atonement, which he considers to be distinctly Pauline in nature. Nettles defines the doctrine in the following way:

> In short, limited atonement affirms that Jesus Christ in dying bore the sins of his people, enduring all the punishment that was due to them by becoming for them the curse that the law demanded . . . all of whom he knew and to whom he was joined before the foundation of the world.[21]

In other words, Christ only died for the elect. There is nothing novel here; Nettles is simply restating this classic Calvinistic doctrine. Interestingly, however, Nettles delineates two separate understandings of limited atonement. First, certain individuals (such as Andrew Fuller) understand the atonement to be sufficient for all, but limited or efficient only for the elect. Second, Nettles (and he cites others such as J. L. Dagg) sides with the understanding that views Christ's atonement as only sufficient for and

---

18. Nettles, *By His Grace and for His Glory*, 256–47.
19. Nettles, *By His Grace and for His Glory*, 267.
20. Nettles, *By His Grace and for His Glory*, 285–87.
21. Nettles, *By His Grace and for His Glory*, 298.

limited to the elect. He is quick, though, to assure his readers that both understandings are consistent within the scope of historic Calvinism.[22]

Nettles concludes his theological exposition by treating the doctrine of perseverance of the saints. He promptly distinguishes between the doctrine of perseverance and "easy believism." This doctrine is no license for sin; rather, it is a test of salvific authenticity. The doctrine of perseverance often reveals the sorrowful state of humanity's self deception (false conversion). Yet, it also proclaims the glory of God's preserving grace (true conversion). To Nettles, the doctrine of perseverance of the saints includes three vital elements: God's preserving the believer, the believer's participation in perseverance, and the fact of the ongoing presence of sin in redeemed humanity.[23]

John Piper

John Piper (1946–) is something of a hero among Reformed Baptists. He is a prolific writer, having authored more than thirty books, and has devoted much scholarly effort to the study and advocacy of Jonathan Edwards. He was raised, the son of a minister, in Greenville, South Carolina. Eventually, his education brought him to such institutions as Wheaton College (B.A., 1968), Fuller Theological Seminary (B.D., 1971), and the University of Munich (Th.D., 1974). Currently, Piper pastors at Bethlehem Baptist Church (BGC) in Minnesota.[24]

Piper is most definitely associated with Dortian Calvinism. In fact, he is known to support seven points of Calvinism, adding reprobation (double predestination) and the "best of all possible worlds" theory to the five.[25] Piper's view on reprobation is seen in his handling of Romans 9:16–18.[26] He argues that the hardening of Pharaoh's heart is active on the part of God (it is not a reaction to sin), and is, consequently, the result of divine reprobation.[27]

---

22. Nettles, *By His Grace and for His Glory*, 302–05.
23. Nettles, *By His Grace and for His Glory*, 322–33.
24. Garrett, *Baptist Theology*, 661.
25. Piper, "What Does Piper Mean," para.1.
26. Piper, *The Justification of God*, 175.
27. Interestingly, Piper differs somewhat with Edwards here. Edwards argues that there is no positive volition on the part of God with regard to the hardening of Pharaoh's heart. God does not put forth any power with the intent of directly hardening the heart. According to Edwards, to assume positive efficiency here would be to "make God the

The doctrines of total depravity and irresistible grace are present within Piper's treatment of missions in *Desiring God*. He insists that the work of missions is humanly impossible as a result of spiritual deadness. Mankind is dead in sin, utterly depraved. Yet, mission work is possible because it is God who conducts this great miracle through the means of human endeavor. It is God's call that ultimately brings conversion. God's call is irresistible because it overpowers spiritual deadness; it is infallible in this way. And so, the work of missions is God's accomplishing the humanly impossible, the conversion of souls.[28]

The notion of God's sovereignty, says Piper, demands that one define election as unconditional. In his dealing with Romans 9, Piper rejects any interpretation that would view God as electing nations rather than persons. This text, argues Piper, reveals God's divine purpose in election. It is God who before all time chose those who would be saved out of Israel. This election is not the result of any behavior on the part of individuals. Instead, it is solely the result of God's divine unconditional purpose or election.[29]

Limited atonement is certainly upheld by Piper as well. He responds in a two-fold manner to the many evangelicals who would think of Christ's atonement as being for all persons. First, he sees, in one sense, this idea as healthy. It is healthy to think of Christ's sacrifice as being available to all who have faith regardless of ethnicity or social standing. Second, Piper views this notion, however, as potentially unhealthy, if one understands Christ's death to have accomplished the same thing for the saved as it did for the lost. He demands that to hold such a view is to fail to embrace fully Christ's covenant love for his bride. Jesus, Piper argues, paid for the sins of his church (the elect) and not for those who are ultimately lost.[30]

Finally, Piper defends the doctrine of perseverance of the saints (eternal security) as biblical. He stresses that those who are truly born again are secure. This does not, however, imply that one who is regenerate may live as though he or she were unregenerate. There is a false sense

---

immediate author of sin." Edwards, *God's Sovereignty in the Salvation of Men*, 2:849.

28. Piper, *Desiring God*, 235.
29. Piper, *The Justification of God*, 175.
30. John Piper, "For Whom Did Jesus Taste Death," Internet.

of security associated with those who think themselves to be in the faith and, yet, live as though they are not.[31]

A CALL FOR BAPTIST DISTINCTIVES

In his treatment of several contemporary Baptists, James Leo Garrett, Jr., after having interacted with John Piper, concludes the following: "John Piper . . . has increasingly demonstrated that he is first evangelical and Reformed and second Baptist."[32] If Garrett's critique is true of this prominent and celebrated figure in Baptist life, then, perhaps, a fresh call or stressing of Baptist distinctives is in order. Malcolm Yarnell argues that there are four divisions which define what it is to be Baptist: a missional focus, a stressing of personal conversion, an upholding of the regenerate church, and biblical authority.[33] The following is a brief discussion of the two most pressing distinctives for the purpose of this paper.[34]

Missions and Evangelism

A focus on missions and evangelism is certainly one key ingredient to the Baptist identity. Andrew Fuller's exegetical approach to the Great Commission—that it was issued to all Christians in all times—was used as an important scriptural proof in order to establish, for his Baptist brethren, that the gospel of Christ must be proclaimed.[35] This focus is

---

31. Piper, *Desiring God*, 196n.

32. Garrett's quote is in the context of Piper having advocated to his congregation (in 2005) an open membership policy. The change in church constitution would have rendered convinced paedobaptists as eligible for church membership. Garrett, *Baptist Theology*, 665–66.

33. Yarnell, "The Heart of a Baptist," 76. Also, it should be noted that D. W. Bebbington's four evangelical distinctives intersect thematically here with Yarnell's Baptist distinctives (the regenerate church being an exception). Bebbington, *Evangelicalism in Modern Britain*, 2–3.

34. The greatest foe of personal conversion and biblical authority is not Reformed theology (and a moderate Calvinism is no foe at all); rather, it is theological liberalism. Personal conversion is irrelevant as a result of liberalism's anthropological optimism (sin is simply ignorance). There are some Reformed scholars (Muller for example) who dislike the language of personal conversion. Nevertheless, the Reformed tradition generally upholds the notion of individual conversion. Also, the liberal anti-supernatural bias does great violence to the authority of the Bible. The Bible is read and critiqued just as any other historical work. Muller, "How Many Points," 430; Ahlstrom, *A Religious History of the American People*, 772–79

35. Validation for this claim may be examined in chapter 4 of this book.

in harmony, historically, with the Anabaptist emphasis and interpretive approach to the Great Commission (Balthasar Hubmaier for example).[36] The Anabaptist emphasis likewise demands that Christ's commission is for all Christians in all eras. This view is in contrast to Calvin's position which assigned the boundless mandate of the Great Commission to the Apostles alone.[37]

And so it was Andrew Fuller (1754–1815) that helped to reestablish this missionary focus as a hallmark for Baptist identity among the Particular Baptists. The eighteenth-century English Particular Baptists are generally regarded as being under the influence of hyper-Calvinism, and John Gill is typically viewed as a leading voice among these hyper-Calvinistic expressions.[38] Now whether Gill was a hyper-Calvinist in practice or not is hotly debated—certain scholars such as Timothy George and Thomas Nettles would defend Gill regarding this charge of hyper-Calvinism.[39] However, few deny that Gill promoted a doctrine of eternal justification, and that this teaching was carried out to its anti-evangelistic logical conclusion.[40] To Gill, justification resides in eternity and not in space and time. It is only the application of active justification for the elect that exists outside of eternity. Consequently, faith does not act as a vehicle for justification; rather, justification is the occasion for faith.[41] It was in this anti-evangelistic environment that Andrew Fuller's *Gospel Worthy of all Acceptation* sounded the siren and ushered in a revival of Baptist missions and evangelism.

The Regenerate Church

The notion of a regenerate church is most assuredly a defining doctrine for the Baptist. The Baptist must never concede that there is a great chasm between the visible and invisible church; instead, one must strive

---

36. For a discussion of Hubmaier's views on the Great Commission, see Yarnell, "The Heart of a Baptist," 74.

37. One must not necessarily presume that Calvin was anti-missions as result of his interpretation of the Great Commission. Chapter 3 contains further details related to this claim.

38. Young, "Andrew Fuller," 17–18.

39. George, "John Gill," 26; Nettles, *By His Grace and for His Glory*, 106–07.

40. For example, Michael Haykin posits a similar claim in his recent paper on the subject. Haykin, "Hyper-Calvinism," 12–15.

41. Gill, *A Body of Doctrinal and Practical Divinity*, 29; George, "John Gill," 26.

to make these two indistinguishable.[42] How, then, is this accomplished? Baptists (as the name suggests) look to believer's baptism, Christ's command for the converted (Matt 28:19). Baptism is a profession of faith; it is a representation of one's conversion and a safeguard for a regenerate visible church.[43]

The visible church should be thought of as a group of regenerate believers gathered for the purpose of fulfilling God's will. And so, it is this notion of a regenerate church that firmly confronts the Reformed understanding of infant baptism. Richard Fuller argues that the practice of infant baptism was an export of Roman error into the Reformers's theology, and that it indirectly promotes the mistruth that the church somehow mechanically pardons its members from sin. Paedobaptism, Fuller continues, reverses the biblical order of conversion and baptism followed by church membership (Acts 2:41, Acts 8:36–38, Acts 10:44–48). The Reformed tradition, through paedobaptism, adds the infants to the church in hopes that they will undergo conversion at a later time.[44]

Other ingredients that ensure and define a regenerate church are continual fellowship with the body of Christ, the Lord's Supper, and submission to church teaching and discipline.[45] It is true that one cannot with certainty ensure perfect unity between the visible and invisible church. Nevertheless, these biblical criteria can be enforced and regarded in such a way that the idea of a regenerate church is preserved as real and legitimate. Furthermore, the implications of certain biblical commands, such as baptism for believers only, demand that the Baptist must uphold and preserve the church as a regenerate body of believers.

FULLERISM AS OPPOSED TO CALVINISM: THE THESIS

The author has argued, in this chapter, that historical and contemporary Baptists have associated themselves with Calvinism. Also, as a result, this chapter has stressed the necessity for Baptist distinctives. The intention, then, of this book will be to examine the theology of Andrew Fuller as a potentially superior model for preserving Baptist doctrine

---

42. Erickson, *Christian Theology*, 1058.
43. Yarnell, "The Heart of a Baptist," 79–80.
44. Fuller, *Baptism and the Terms of Communion*, 215–24.
45. Dever, "The Doctrine of the Church," 840; Yarnell, "The Heart of a Baptist," 80.

and practice, particularly for those who hold to what is referred to as a Reformed soteriology. Consequently, this project will examine whether it is more appropriate for such Baptists to be regarded as Fullerites rather than Calvinists.

Certainly, with regard to ecclesiology, the Reformed tradition in many ways is in direct opposition to Baptist convictions. But, it will be the focus of this paper to question if Calvin's missiology is lacking at times when compared to Baptist theological moorings. For example, many have argued that historic Reformed missiology is underdeveloped at best. Some have gone so far as to say that the Reformers (including Calvin) actually lacked missionary zeal. Scholars often ascribe this lack of missiological focus to the Reformers's own peculiar historical context.[46] Even if Calvin's missiology is simply underdeveloped, this may be reason enough for Baptists to seek out a more thorough theological system.

Certainly, matters pertaining to soteriology and ecclesiology logically intersect when discussing the doctrine of missions. For example, when Fuller's soteriology is compared to Calvin's and the Reformed tradition in general (understood most clearly through the template of Dortian Calvinism), many similarities are apparent. Nevertheless, there are some subtle soteriological distinctions that seem to have more profound missiological implications.[47] When a diligent examination of these matters is complete, a conclusion will be presented as to whether common designations such as "Calvinist" and "Reformed" are helpful when applied to Baptist doctrinal systems.

---

46. Anderson, "Medieval and Renaissance Missions," 194–95.

47. For instance, Fuller's "New Light" or "Edwardsian" distinction between natural and moral ability is a subtle shift from more traditional Calvinism. Garrett, *Baptist Theology*, 182.

2

Historical Survey

THE AFFILIATION BETWEEN BAPTISTS and Calvinism is certainly not a historical anomaly. As has been previously stated, Baptists have a long tradition of agreement with Calvinism, as it relates to soteriology. This Reformed tendency in Baptist history is most clearly seen in the development of the seventeenth-century English Particular Baptists and their descendants. Many of these Baptists held strictly to the five points of Dortian Calvinism; yet, with bravery and conviction they maintained their doctrinal distinctness in areas of ecclesiology,[1] which was seemingly the result of other non-Reformed influences.

It is important, before proceeding, to point out here that the Particular Baptists had the (sometimes neglected) General Baptists as an important counterpart in Baptist history.[2] The General Baptists, whose origins are connected to the person of John Smyth (1570–1612), represent a tradition of Baptist expression that is commonly known for its Arminian theological persuasion.[3] Not only did these men fight against the conventions of their day for Baptist ecclesiology, they also fought against what they thought to be the dangers of Reformed soteriology.

For example, Thomas Grantham (1634–1692) was a General Baptist minister—elected to the office of messenger in 1666—who fre-

---

1. This paper will argue later that Andrew Fuller helped establish missiology (as contemporary Baptists understand it) as another distinct feature of Baptist identity.

2. Stephen Wright has argued against the traditional view that seventeenth-century Baptists were initially divided, as a result of soteriological differences, into two distinct denominations (General and Particular). Rather, these early Baptists coexisted, Wright argues, within the framework of more provisional divisions based on issues related to church formation. According to Wright, more permanent denominational lines would not be forged until the publication of the 1644 *London Confession*. Wright, *The Early English Baptists*, 110.

3. McBeth, *The Baptist Heritage*, 32.

quently wrote and labored on behalf of his Baptist brethren.[4] Grantham, in his work entitled *A Dialogue between the Baptist and the Presbyterian*, strongly resists Reformed soteriology. In this writing, Grantham seems to be most concerned with what he fears to be the implications of Calvinism regarding sin (Calvinism makes God the author of sin) and the atonement (limited atonement as an impediment to evangelism).[5] This chapter, however, is concerned with the historical connection between Baptists and the extent of their association with Reformed theology. Consequently, the remaining discussion will focus on the Particular Baptists, their influences, and a brief treatment of Andrew Fuller.

THE PARTICULAR BAPTISTS

The English Particular Baptists emerged into conscious distinction through the publication of *The London Confession* in 1644.[6] These noble and devout believers represent a true landmark in Baptist and free church history. Though many of these Baptist leaders did not have the formal training of their state church contemporaries, they, nevertheless, wrote with clarity and a passion for biblical truth. Stanley Nelson notes that the Particular Baptists in their 1646 revised confession admitted to being ignorant in some respects and desired to learn. Nelson interprets this admission as an acknowledgment of these Baptists's self awareness regarding their lack of education, and that for this reason they used outside sources to develop their Confession. Observe the following:

> These men were aware that they did not possess the formal training of their peers . . . The confession writers' situation seemed pathetically small in the light of that national assembly. For these and perhaps other reasons, the writers turned to other sources to aid them in setting forth their beliefs.[7]

This author would like to suggest an alternative interpretation for the unassuming words of these early Particular Baptists. Rather than some sort of self deprecating timidity, these Baptist leaders were exhibiting

---

4. It has been argued that Grantham is the first Baptist to deliver a systematic theology in the writing of his *Christianismus Primitivus*. Garrett, *Baptist Theology*, 42.

5. Mauldin, "Transcriber's Preface to A Dialogue between the Baptist and the Presbyterian," 185.

6. White, *The English Baptists*, 59.

7. Nelson, "Reflecting on Baptist Origins," 34.

a true sense of Christian humility. If any apologist (or persecutor as it were) had been able to provide these men with persuasive biblical refutations, they would have surely recanted their error. And it is this passion for God's word and humility that sets the tone for this important era in Baptist history.

These early English Baptists, some have argued, descended from a moderate form of separatism.[8] The clearly apologetic appeal of the 1644 confession may lend credence to these remnants of semi-separatism. The confession intended to set right several misunderstandings regarding the Particular Baptists. Essentially, by providing a detailed doctrinal confession, these Baptists could allay any notion of similarity with or connection to the lawless expressions of the radical reformation. Also, they would, through the publication of their confession, be able to display the many ways in which their soteriology was in agreement with the prevailing Calvinism of the day.[9]

The "mother church" of these Particular Baptists, which was founded in 1616 in London, is commonly known as the JLJ church, named after its first three pastors (Henry Jacob, John Lathrop, and Henry Jessey).[10] The JLJ church was a Congregationalist Separatist or semi-Separatist body. There was an ongoing discussion within the church regarding the doctrine of baptism and, consequently, the validity of the Church of England. As a result of this ongoing debate, there were several groups throughout the years that left the JLJ church in order to form separate congregations. It is from these congregations that the first Particular Baptist churches emerged.[11]

It is possible that the first Particular Baptist church was founded in 1633, led by Samuel Eaton. This group separated from the "mother church" in order to receive an additional baptism. However, it is unclear as to whether this separation was a rejection of the baptism administered by the Church of England or a rejection of infant baptism in general.[12]

---

8. As time continued, the Particular Baptists certainly did begin to represent a stronger form of separatism. Nevertheless, the JLJ church (the congregation from which the Particular Baptists came) maintained, largely, that the Church of England was a true church in some sense (there were some members, however, who disagreed). McBeth, *The Baptist Heritage*, 39.

9. William L. Lumpkin, *Baptist Confessions of Faith*, 144, 150.

10. McBeth, *The Baptist Heritage*, 42–43.

11. Underwood, *A History of the English Baptists*, 57; White, *The English Baptists*, 60.

12. Jason Duesing provides a helpful rehearsal of the three prominent modern in-

But there is no question as to the position of the 1638 group who left the JLJ church to join John Spilsbury. These believers were most definitely an antipedobaptist church, and, consequently, John Spilsbury's congregation, founded in 1638, is commonly regarded as the first Particular Baptist church.[13]

Also, the traditional argument is that the Particular Baptists led among the historical Baptists in recovering immersion as the proper mode of baptism.[14] Richard Blunt was among those in 1640 who became convinced that a correct doctrine of baptism was not only in affirming its proper recipients as believers but also in affirming immersion as its proper mode (representing death, burial, and resurrection). Consequently, Blunt traveled to the Netherlands (he spoke Dutch) in 1641 in order to investigate a group referred to as the "Collegiants," who were connected to the Mennonites and practiced baptism by immersion. Upon his return, Blunt and a Mr. Blacklock baptized many church members—the result of which further established immersion as standard among the English Baptists, as is evidenced in article 40 of the 1644 confession.[15] It now seems appropriate to devote a small space to two representative figures among the early Particular Baptists.

John Spilsbury

John Spilsbury (1593–1662/68) is an important formative figure among the Particular Baptists. As was mentioned, he was the pastor of the original Particular Baptist church and, as a result, has been rightly referred to as a pioneer. Spilsbury was a cobbler by trade in London. His lack

---

terpretations regarding this historical event, see Duesing, "Counted Worthy," 123–41.

13. Underwood, *A History of the English Baptists*, 58.

14. As a result of ambiguity within the primary historical texts used to support the traditional account of the Baptists's recovery of immersion, Wright again offers an alternative view here. Rather than Richard Blunt consulting with the Collegiant Jan Batten while in the Netherlands, Wright suggests the possibility of Timothy Batte as Blunt's consultant. Batte was a Baptist figure connected to Thomas Lamb, both of whom are associated with the General Baptist tradition. The implication of this proposal is that immersion was not adopted, in the same basic time frame, by two distinct and separate denominations. Instead, in connection with one another, the General and Particular Baptist congregations at this time (being less strictly divided as is traditionally understood) both embraced baptism by immersion. Wright, *The Early English Baptists*, 75–110; for the traditional account, see McBeth, *The Baptist Heritage*, 44.

15. Underwood, *A History of the English Baptists*, 58–59; Lumpkin, *Baptist Confessions of Faith*, 167.

of formal education for the ministry was used as a point of attack by his opponents. However, Spilsbury was certainly not unlearned. In a time when Baptist convictions were often met with violent reactions, Spilsbury's polemical writings provided the English Calvinistic Baptists with an important and well reasoned defense.[16]

Spilsbury's first publication was an apologetic work against paedobaptism entitled *A Treatise Concerning the Lawfull Subject of Baptisme*. The production of this work shows Spilsbury's courage here. He expresses within the writing that his labors had placed his own life in danger. Nevertheless, Spilsbury made several bold arguments for the practice of believer's baptism in his historic work. First, he spent time answering objections to the rejection of paedobaptism.[17] For example, Spilsbury modified covenant theology (though not rejecting it) as he refuted the notion of infant baptism. He argued that the old covenant did not extend to the new covenant's positive ordinances, and that believer's baptism was ordered by Christ and is, therefore, harmonious with the character of the new covenant. Second, Spilsbury rejected the claim that the Baptists's new baptism was negated as a result of a breach in apostolic succession. He argued that Christ's mandate to baptize, as revealed in Scripture, is utterly sufficient in authorizing the reinstatement of true biblical baptism.[18]

Spilsbury also published two essays under the same main title, *God's Ordinance*. The first essay contains Spilsbury's arguments against the Seeker group who denied, as a result of a break in apostolic succession, that there was any true church on earth and that a restoration could only happen with the occurrence of a new Pentecost. The second essay is a treatment in support of limited or particular atonement. Spilsbury maintained that to reject particular atonement would likely lead to devastating outcomes such as a denial of divine predestination and a lack of assurance of perseverance.[19] John Spilsbury does not, perhaps, receive as much current attention as some of his more popular contemporaries; yet, his eminently practical writings and leadership served quite well the young and fragile Particular Baptists of the late 1630s and beyond.

16. For details of John Spilsbury, see Renihan, "John Spilsbury," 21–22; Nettles, *Beginnings in Britain*, 126.
17. Renihan, "John Spilsbury," 26–27.
18. Nettles, *Beginnings in Britain*, 113–14.
19. Reniham, "John Spilsbury," 32–36.

FULLERISM AS OPPOSED TO CALVINISM

William Kiffin

This chapter will consider one further early Particular Baptist, William Kiffin (1616–1701). Kiffin was a signatory of the 1644 *London Confession* and was for this reason, and many others, an important figure in Baptist history.[20] At age nine, Kiffin suffered the profound tragedy of losing both parents to the plague. In fact, he was himself a victim of the plague; yet, God, Kiffin later affirmed, remarkably rescued him from death. In 1629 Kiffin began an apprenticeship (under John Liburne, a Porter Brewer and Cooper in London) of a burdensome nature—as it has been described. He labored hard, nevertheless, for many years, and by the early 1640s Kiffin, as a result of starting his own merchant business, began to accumulate a fortune in personal wealth.[21]

Kiffin's conversion took place in his teenage years. It seems this spiritual transformation was a result of attending sermons from various Puritan ministers. By twenty-two, Kiffin had joined the independent church led by John Lathrop (JLJ church), and in the early 1640s he established a Particular Baptist congregation located at Devonshire Square. Kiffin faithfully labored as pastor of this church for the remainder of his life.[22]

Kiffin's impact on the early Particular Baptists was significant. For example, his wealth and influence provided the platform for Kiffin to aid his fellow Baptists in times of woe.[23] Kiffin was also quite engaged in many of the theological discussions and controversies that weighed heavily on the Baptists in this era. One such controversy was a debate in which Kiffin and three other Baptists, argued against Daniel Featley (an apologist for the Church of England) and his adherence to infant baptism. In keeping with a baptistic focus, Kiffin's argument centered on the scriptural support for believer's baptism. He simply maintained that the baptism of infants was contrary to the clear teaching of the Word of God. Kiffin also argued against Featley for the biblical mode of baptism, immersion.[24]

The internal Baptist debate regarding communion is another issue in which Kiffin made a memorable contribution. For instance, Kiffin

20. White, *The English Baptists*, 70.
21. Wilson, "William Kiffin," 65–66.
22. Nettles, *Beginnings in Britain*, 130–32.
23. Wilson, "William Kiffin," 70.
24. Wilson, "William Kiffin," 71–72; White, *The English Baptists*, 73.

and John Bunyan carried on a written debate for years that centered on baptism's impact on communion (open or closed) and church membership. Kiffin (whose views are reflected in the 1646 edition of the *London Confession*) affirmed the closed communion view. Closed communion allows only believers having been baptized by immersion to participate in the Lord's Supper. Bunyan (whose church practiced open communion and open membership) argued that turning a genuine Christian away from the communion table and from membership, simply because he or she had not received believer's baptism, is to reject those whom God has accepted. Kiffin's response was essentially to emphasize the New Testament pattern, baptism precedes communion. According to Kiffin, to ignore biblical prescriptions in small increments would only lead to larger Popish extra-biblical practices.[25]

Kiffin's influence was quite substantial. In addition to his key involvement in the formation of the original Particular Baptist churches and his participation in the writing of their 1644 confession, Kiffin used his great wealth and influence for good. Kiffin, instead of hording his wealth, used his material gain in order to relieve the suffering of his Baptist brethren. He also, at great risk to his own person, employed his political and social standing to plead for the Baptist cause.[26]

PARTICULAR BAPTIST INFLUENCES

If one is to consider the appropriateness of a theological descriptor (such as Calvinism in this case) as it relates to a Christian movement, then the influences upon that movement must be weighed. Consequently, this section is intended to probe the different persuasions that bore an influence upon the early English Particular Baptists. And, since the *London Confession* of 1644 contains the ingredients for understanding Particular Baptist influences, this document and its sources will be the primary focus of this section.

Menno Simons's Influence

Menno Simons (1496–1561) was a brave Dutch Anabaptist minister who lived and labored in the sixteenth century. In 1524, prior to his conversion to Anabaptist convictions, Simons was a Catholic priest in

---

25. McBeth, *The Baptist Heritage*, 81–83.
26. Wilson, "William Kiffin," 72.

the village of Pingjum. Also, Simons, in 1525, began to struggle with the Catholic doctrine of transubstantiation (which was not uncommon during this time). And, of course, Simons's struggle with infant baptism undoubtedly helped to shape his evangelical conscience. He reports that consulting the writings of Luther, Bullinger, Bucer, and even his own Catholic tradition proved unfruitful in harmonizing paedobaptism with scripture.[27]

The catalyst, however, for Simons to act upon his new convictions (that is to leave the Catholic church) was the infamous Münster revolution. This group of rogue, violent Anabaptists represents only a small piece or fringe group of the Anabaptist heritage. Sadly, Simons (a pacifist) would spend much of his life trying to repel the lasting memories of these violent revolutionaries. After the Münster revolution, Simons was moved to act upon his convictions and provide the much needed spiritual leadership, teaching, and unifying theological direction to a growing group of wandering sheep. It would now be impossible for him to "escape the cross of Christ."[28] This decision was indeed a bearing of the cross for Simons. He would endure eighteen years as a hunted man, laboring for the gospel of Christ with his family. Fortunately, Simons was allowed for the last several years of his life to live and work in peace on the estate of a sympathizing nobleman in North Germany.[29]

Simons's most significant and distributed writing is his 1539 *Foundation of Christian Doctrine*.[30] The author is proposing, for the reasons stated below, that this important writing of Simons's was a source (as it regards baptism) for the Particular Baptists as they prepared their 1644 confession. This position has been convincingly argued by Glen Stassen in two separate scholarly articles.[31] The evidence for this is observed when one compares the terminology, order of themes, and identical scriptural references between Simons's book and articles 39 and 40 of the 1644 confession.

---

27. Simons, *Reply to Gellius Faber*, Works 668–69; Voolstra, "*Menno Simons,*" 363.

28. Simons, *The Foundation of Christian Doctrine*, Works 669–70.

29. Lane, *A Concise History of Christian Thought*, 191.

30. Wenger, introduction to "The Foundation of Christian Doctrine," by Menno Simons, Works 104.

31. Stassen, "Anabaptist Influence," 322–48. Stassen also provides, in a more recent treatment, further evidence to support his thesis; see Stassen, "Opening Menno Simons's Foundation-Book," 34–44.

To begin, Simons (using Matt 28:18–19 and Mark 16:16) refers to baptism as an "ordinance of God" and states that it should only be administered to those who believe.[32] Likewise, the Baptists began article 39 of their confession by asserting that "Baptisme is an Ordinance of the New Testament" intended for those "professing faith," while employing the very same scriptural references as Simons.[33] Other sources of influence for the Baptists (the *True Confession* for example) used the term "sacrament" rather than "ordinance" to categorize or refer to baptism.[34]

Another striking similarity is the way Simons and the Baptists describe baptism as an indicator of a profession of faith. After quoting Acts 2:37 and Acts 8:37, Simons declares, "Faith does not follow from baptism, but baptism follows from faith." Later Simons insists that baptism represents a profession of faith.[35] This language is also detected in the 1644 confession (article 39) when it speaks of baptism being suitable only for those "persons professing faith." And, in keeping with the apparent pattern, the Baptists seem to have included Simons's scriptural references as they provided biblical validation for their views (Acts 2:37–38, 8:36–38, and 18:8).[36]

The last textual similarity to be discussed here is Simons's and the Baptists's common focus on baptism being a representation of the death, burial, and resurrection of Jesus. Simons reveals this representational focus of baptism by expounding Paul's text in Romans 6:3–5.[37] The Baptists, likewise, affirm the same symbolic meaning of baptism, using the very same scriptural citation, in article 40 of their confession.[38] It is worth mentioning that while Simons does use the phrase "immersing in water" (*Indruckinge in't Water*), he did not practice baptism by immersion.[39] This fact, however, does not seem to be any great mark against the case for Anabaptist influence upon Particular Baptists. First, Simons's text here does read as though he promoted immersion (grammatically speaking). And second, even if the Baptists knew that Simons

---

32. Simons, *The Foundation of Christian Doctrine*, Works 120.
33. Lumpkin, *Baptist Confessions of Faith*, 167.
34. Stassen, "Opening Menno Simons's Foundation-Book," 34–44.
35. Simons, *The Foundation of Christian Doctrine*, Works 120.
36. Lumpkin, *Baptist Confessions of Faith*, 167.
37. Simons, *The Foundation of Christian Doctrine*, Works 122.
38. Lumpkin, *Baptist Confessions of Faith*, 167
39. Simons, *The Foundation of Christian Doctrine*, Works 123, 123n.

did not practice immersion (which is likely since Simons later in this work describes baptism in a way other than immersion), they, being competent theological thinkers, were certainly capable of modifying Simons's thinking in a manner that represented the further light which they had received.

An additional consideration regarding Stassen's theory focuses on the accessibility of Simons's Dutch document to these Baptist Englishmen. In other words, could these Baptists have been able to obtain and translate a Dutch writing such as that of Simons's? This can be answered by remembering that Richard Blunt, the early Particular Baptist leader, spoke Dutch and in fact traveled in 1641 to confer with Dutch Mennonites (and perhaps Timothy Batte) regarding baptism by immersion.[40] This seems, then, adequate in establishing the possibility for Particular Baptist access to Simons's *Foundation of Christian Doctrine*.

James Renihan represents one scholarly objection to Stassen's theory. Renihan acknowledges the close pattern between Simons's work and the 1644 confession. However, he accuses Stassen of overstatement. Essentially, Renihan argues that the reality of Simons's non-immersion practice is a detriment to Stassen's Anabaptist influence theory.[41] Also, as a result of the death, burial, and resurrection motif employed by Simons and the Baptists, Stassen argues, to a large extent, there was an elimination of the ordinance being understood as regeneration by washing. Renihan asserts that Stassen's observation here is somewhat bloated. He insists that the 1644 confession significantly incorporates both symbolic meanings: death, burial, and resurrection as well as regeneration by washing.[42] As a result of these critiques, Renihan, interestingly, points to Praise God Barebone and his *A Discourse Tending to Prove the Baptisme in, or under The Defection of Antichrist to be the Ordinance of Jesus Christ*, as an alternative source for the Particular Baptists in the writing of their 1644 confession.[43] This is a curious theory since Barebone's work was against

---

40. Stassen, "Anabaptist Influence," 326–27. Also, see Stephen Wright on Timothy Batte and his possible influence upon Richard Blunt. Wright, *The Early English Baptists*, 75–110.

41. As was previously stated, these Baptists seem eminently capable of modifying Simons's non-immersion practice and, yet, still employ the remainder of his doctrinal template as it regards baptism.

42. Renihan, "An Examination of the Possible Influence of Menno Simons' Foundation Book," 198–99.

43. Renihan, "An Examination of the Possible Influence of Menno Simons'

the "innovative" practice of the Baptists. Nevertheless, even if one were to concede that the Baptists's 1644 confession (in articles 39 and 40) was a response to Barebone, this in no way excludes the Baptists from having used Simons's *Foundation Book* as a source for their rebuttal.

Calvinist Influences

This section will now focus its attention on the aspect of Particular Baptist origins which are virtually undisputed. It seems impossible to ignore Reformed theology's influence upon the English Particular Baptists and their descendants. John Briggs notes in his article that "Seventeenth-century Baptists were essentially Reformed or Calvinistic Christians who admitted believers, on the declaration of their faith in baptism, into congregationally ordered churches."[44] While this quote unintentionally or inadvertently admits a significant modification to certain aspects within Reformed theology,[45] Calvinism's effect upon Baptists, particularly in the area of soteriology, is a point which must surely be conceded. It is commonly understood that the 1644 confession writers used significant portions of the 1596 *True Confession* (a Reformed Congregationalist document), as well as having made use of *The Marrow of Theology* (the systematic theology written by William Ames, the monumental English Puritan).[46]

So then, where can Calvinism be found in the 1644 *London Confession*? To begin, article 3 articulates a version of the doctrine of unconditional election: "God had in Christ before the foundation of the world, according to the good pleasure of his will, foreordained some men to eternall life . . ."[47] But, this affirmation of divine election did not necessitate, to these Baptists, a strict doctrine of reprobation. And, it is here that one may note the difference between Dortian Calvinism and Calvinism proper (Calvinism being the teaching of John Calvin). For example, in article 3, the Baptist confession avoids the language of rep-

---

Foundation Book," 200–02.

44. Briggs, "The Influence of Calvinism," 10.

45. Clearly, the rejection of infant baptism is a modification of covenant theology, which, in this author's estimation, should not be glossed over. The necessity of volition on the part of the baptismal candidate is certainly a qualification to certain aspects of Calvinism or Reformed doctrine, see Nelson, "Reflecting on Baptist Origins," 43.

46. Stassen, "Opening Menno Simons's Foundation-Book," 34.

47. Lumpkin, *Baptist Confessions of Faith*, 157.

robation: "leaving the rest in their sinne to their just condemnation..."[48] This language appears to lack direct volition and falls under the category of what Garrett would call preterition.[49] In this way, the Baptists, in their confession, were more in line with the language found in the Synod of Dort than with Calvin himself.

To illustrate, article 15 of chapter 1 in the *Synod of Dort* asserts that some men are "non-elect, or *passed by* in the eternal election of God..."[50] In other words, humankind is not (in a direct sense) elected unto damnation or reprobated.[51] Such a person is, rather, passed over or left to pay the consequences of willful sin. There is an element of passivity here (with the Baptists and with Dort) that is certainly distinct from Calvin's teaching. Charles Partee (an excellent contemporary interpreter of Calvin) concludes that Calvin clearly affirms damnation as the result of God having elected or predestined individual persons to such a state.[52] Note Calvin's affirmation from his *Institutes*, in the following quote:

> As Scripture, then, clearly shows, we say that God once established by his eternal and unchangeable plan those whom he long before determined once for all to receive into salvation, and those whom, on the other hand, he would devote to destruction. We assert that, with respect to the elect, this plan was founded upon his freely given mercy... by his just and irreprehensible but incomprehensible judgment he has barred the door of life to those whom he has given over to damnation... But as the Lord seals his elect by call and justification, so, by shutting off the reprobate from knowledge of his name or from the sanctification from his Spirit, he, as it were, reveals by these marks what sort of judgment awaits them.[53]

The early Particular Baptists in their 1644 confession, while affirming divine unconditional election, made a conscious effort to avoid this sort of strict doctrine of reprobation.

Article 5 in the 1644 *London Confession* describes for its readers the Reformed doctrine of total depravity. Humankind is described as

---

48. Lumpkin, *Baptist Confessions of Faith*, 157.
49. Garrett, *Systematic Theology*, 2:443–47.
50. Scott, trans., *The Articles of the Synod of Dort*, 188.
51. The *Synod of Dort* at least avoids the language of strict reprobation.
52. Partee, *The Theology of John Calvin*, 249.
53. Calvin, *Institutes*, 3.21.7.

"altogether dead in sinnes." It is because of this woeful state that humanity is totally dependent upon the free grace of God Almighty. Because lost humanity is utterly dead in sin, God's great salvation must never be considered a work of man. Rather, it must only be recognized as a work wholly of God.[54]

The atonement of Christ is limited to the elect only, according to articles 17 and 21 of the 1644 confession. God gave to Christ those who would be saved, and it is this elect for whom Christ's death was intended. The Baptist writers, however, are quick to insist upon the necessity of preaching the gospel to all men.[55] Also, those persons saved by Christ, through his atoning work on the cross, are never finally lost. This teaching of perseverance is clear in article 23 of the confession. The Baptists here were certain to ensure that this doctrine was not understood as a license for sin. Rather, true Christians are those who can never be removed from the "foundation and rock which by faith they are fastened upon."[56]

Finally, Briggs points out that the seventeenth-century Baptists, like the Reformed tradition and the reformers in general, clung tightly to the doctrine of *sola scriptura*—a doctrine that was revived in the Protestant Reformation.[57] Granted, in this way the early Particular Baptists were influenced by Reformed theology. However, this author argues that these Baptists applied this doctrine in a significantly more thorough manner. One example (touched on before) is the fact that Baptists were driven by their biblical exegesis to the doctrine of believers's baptism by immersion. The rejection of infant baptism was not an unimportant or peripheral modification to covenant theology.[58] Covenantal paedobaptism is, it can be argued, a philosophically driven hermeneutic (more deductive in nature) rather than a more inductive biblically driven hermeneutic. Consequently, as it regards baptism, these English Baptists, one might

---

54. Lumpkin, *Baptist Confessions of Faith*, 158.
55. Lumpkin, *Baptist Confessions of Faith*, 160, 162.
56. Lumpkin, *Baptist Confessions of Faith*, 163.
57. Briggs, "The Influence of Calvinism," 10.
58. Apparently, Muller would agree that infant baptism is no small component to Reformed or covenant theology. Muller's argument regarding this is discussed in chapter 1 of this book. While this writer does not agree with some of Muller's conclusions, it is still, nevertheless, important to note that many within the Reformed tradition understand doctrines such as infant baptism to be fundamentally bound up in the Reformed theological system. See Muller, "How Many Points," 425–433.

observe, were more ardent in their application of *sola scriptura* than their Reformed counterparts.[59]

Another example of seventeenth-century Baptists altering their Reformed influences is found in their rejection of the doctrine of preparationism. Preparationism is a common feature among English and American Reformed Puritans. As has been established, the writers of the 1644 confession were certainly influenced by English Puritanism (William Ames being one clear example). The doctrine of preparationism can be defined as a highly developed, pre-salvific, standardized, consistent progression that an individual undergoes in order to be made ready for Christ, which may or may not result in regeneration. Several generic stages can be listed providing a general overview of the process: observance of the ministry of the word, an awareness of the law, a keen sense of one's sin, and a holy sense of terror.[60] Among the activities one engages throughout the process of preparation is the casting away of sin.[61] Now the 1644 confession writers flatly deny preparationism. Observe their words in article 25: "The tenders of the Gospel to the conversion of sinners, is absolutely free, no way requiring . . . any qualifications, preparations, terrors of the law, or preceding ministry of the law, but onely and alone the naked soule, as a sinner and ungodly to receive Christ."[62] So then, the early Particular Baptists were influenced by Reformed theology in many respects and Anabaptism in other respects (as demonstrated in the previous section). Yet, these influences were in no way without qualification and were undoubtedly subject to the Word of God.

---

59. Malcolm Yarnell discusses the idea that the Protestants, while claiming scripture alone, did in fact move away from strictly biblical foundations in certain respects. Yarnell, *The Formation of Christian Doctrine*, 112.

60. Morgan, *Visible Saints*, 68–69.

61. This is a literal pre-salvific denial of sinful behavior. This, as well as other activities, is regarded as working the means of grace. It is true, the Puritans developed this teaching into the sophisticated nuanced doctrine that it is. However, traces of this thought are found in the Synod of Dort as well. The Synod addresses those who might be in despair, thinking they are, perhaps, reprobate. These persons are told, among other things, to be diligent in working the means of grace. Ames, *The Marrow of Theology*, 160; Scott, trans., *The Articles of the Synod of Dort*, 188–89.

62. Lumpkin, *Baptist Confessions of Faith*, 163.

ANDREW FULLER

As a direct descendent of the early Particular Baptists and as the key Baptist figure in this paper's doctrinal comparison, a section on the life and ministry of Andrew Fuller (1754–1815) is appropriate. Such a section is also needful since Fuller's life and contributions are less known and less celebrated by the wider Christian community than many of his Protestant Reformed counterparts. What follows below, then, is a brief biographical sketch highlighting some of Fuller's major contributions.

Fuller was born in 1754 and subsequently spent his childhood in Wicken, Cambridgeshire, England. His parents were farmers, dissenting and Baptist in their convictions.[63] Fuller describes his church experience, essentially, as irrelevant to the unconverted. In other words, gospel calls from the pulpit were nonexistent in Fuller's childhood congregation. He further portrays his family's minister as being "tinged with false Calvinism."[64] And so, it is in this environment (high or hyper-Calvinistic) that Fuller grew up, later coming to faith in Christ in spite of his minister's neglect of the gospel mandate.

Fuller's spiritual journey to salvation is detailed in his memoirs. He begins by describing himself as a child with only transient convictions. There were only passing or fleeting seasons of guilt over sin for Fuller. In the main, he was quite unhampered in his life of transgression. Fuller describes, though, times in his life when, upon reading books like *Pilgrim's Progress*, he would be overcome with conviction. Yet, as a result of hyper-Calvinism's influence, Fuller did not sense that he had experienced a true "warrant of faith" (an inner conviction that one was among the elect). So, it would not be until his sixteenth year (1769) that Fuller finally came to a true saving knowledge of Christ. He describes himself as having an unusually heavy burden with regard to his sin. He was so burdened that he began to despair of his eternal fate. Fuller knew with certainty that as a result of his sin, God would be perfectly right in exercising his holy justice. It was at this point that the knowledge of the gospel of grace rang true in Fuller's heart. He rejected his past life of sin and began his life as a committed and humble servant of Christ.[65]

---

63. Roberts, "Andrew Fuller," 35.
64. Fuller, *Memoir*, Works 1:2.
65. Fuller, *Memoir*, Works 1:2–6; Morden, *Offering Christ to the World*, 27–28.

In 1770 Fuller was baptized and received as a member of the Baptist church at Soham. By 1775, the young Andrew Fuller was made pastor there at his home church. He continued for some years in the high or hyper-Calvinism which was common in his day. However, in 1781 several elements began to move Fuller toward the evangelical Calvinism for which he is famous.[66] Garrett describes four such influential elements upon Fuller: First, he began to read books written in favor of an evangelical Calvinism. Second, he studied key scriptural texts leading him away from hyper-Calvinistic principles. Third, he observed the success of missionary preaching from such men as David Brainerd. Fourth, Fuller began to read the new light Calvinism of Jonathan Edwards, Sr.[67] The result of this theological wrestling was that Fuller came to believe, promote, and practice the indiscriminate preaching of the gospel. One may observe the details of Fuller's new theological conviction in his 1785 publication, *The Gospel Worthy of all Acceptation*.[68]

Beginning in 1784, Fuller (now pastoring in Kettering) was among several particular Baptist ministers (which would later include William Carey) who desired to organize a missionary society. It was not, however, until 1792 that the Baptist Missionary Society would officially be formed. William Carey preached his famous sermon at the annual association meeting. In this sermon, Carey made an impassioned call for service unto God. The influence of Carey's sermon, among other factors, eventually led to the planning of a new missionary organization. Fuller would become the chief administrator of this young missionary society. He would spend the rest of his life laboring for the missionaries under his care. Fuller was also the great defender and theologian for this young missionary movement.[69] So, it is Andrew Fuller, one of the fathers of the modern missions movement, who provided an appropriate theological rationale for future missionary endeavor.

In conclusion, this chapter has provided the majority of the historical context needed to pursue this book's thesis question. Of course, the remaining chapters will necessarily contain some historical discussion. Nevertheless, much of what follows will be theological in nature, namely, analyzing the missiologies of John Calvin and Andrew Fuller.

66. Roberts, "Andrew Fuller," 36.
67. Garrett, *Baptist Theology*, 175–76.
68. Roberts, "Andrew Fuller," 36.
69. Young, "Andrew Fuller," 18–22.

3

Doctrinal Study of John Calvin

JOHN CALVIN, IT HAS been argued, is the most important systematic theologian among the Protestant Reformers.¹ His influence even to this day can hardly be exaggerated. Although, for all the scholarly study that his teaching enjoys, he is, perhaps, one of the more misunderstood persons in church history. This may be illustrated by acknowledging the fact that his name is often evoked (Calvinism) when describing any number of related, yet, distinct theological systems. This chapter, then, will attempt to help clarify (at least in the area of missions) some of Calvin's doctrinal teaching.

The subject of missions as it relates to John Calvin (or the Protestant Reformers in general) has received much attention throughout the years.² When approaching a study of this nature, several questions arise: Did Calvin's soteriology impact his missiology negatively? Did Calvin lack missionary zeal? Did Calvin have an underdeveloped missiology or perhaps no discernable missiology at all? This chapter intends to cover these and other questions by organizing its discussion under several broad headings. The first heading, in order to provide context, will consist of a brief biographical treatment of Calvin. Second, it should also prove helpful to present a survey of the prevailing sentiments regarding the Reformers and missions. The third heading will be an attempt to present a balanced and more broadly informed view of Calvin's missiology (or role in missions) than is often posited. Finally, this chapter will humbly argue that Calvin's missiology was malformed as a result of two important factors.

---

1. Gonzalez, *The Story of Christianity*, 2:61.

2. Many of the sources to be cited later in this chapter will adequately establish this assertion.

BIOGRAPHICAL DATA

John Calvin was born on July 10, 1509 in the small French town of Noyon. His father was secretary to a Bishop in the church, and, as a result of his father's connections, Calvin received (in his twelfth year) an ecclesiastical scholarship for his studies.[3] Traditionally, Calvin is said to have begun his studies in philosophy in Paris by age fourteen. It is interesting to note here, however, that Alister McGrath is quite suspicious of this accepted timeline for Calvin's university studies in Paris.[4] He cites the meager documentation commonly employed to construct the history of Calvin's early career. Nevertheless, after 1528 Calvin shifted his focus of study to law, which was conducted in Orleans and Bourges. In addition to law, Calvin also, under the tutelage of the Humanist Wolmar, was given the opportunity to study classic writers such as Homer and Demosthenes as well as the Greek New Testament. Calvin rapidly came to be recognized as extraordinary among his professors and fellow students alike.[5]

The details of Calvin's conversion to Christianity (or at least to Protestant Christianity) are somewhat lacking. Perhaps Calvin was influenced by his Humanist professors or through his study of the Greek New Testament.[6] Little is known here except that there was in fact a point of departure with respect to Roman sympathies. Note Calvin in the following:

> God, by the secret guidance of his providence, at length gave a different direction to my course. And first, since I was too obstinately devoted to the superstitions of Popery to be easily extricated from so profound an abyss of mire, God by a sudden conversion subdued and brought my mind to a teachable frame . . .[7]

In 1534, Calvin forfeited his ecclesiastical posts and the funding that accompanied them.[8] And, it was also in this year that Francis I shifted

---

3. Gonzalez, *The Story of Christianity*, 2:61–63.

4. For a detailed discussion of this argument, see McGrath, *A Life of John Calvin*, 21–22.

5. Newman, *A Manual of Church History*, 2:203–04.

6. Gonzalez, *The Story of Christianity*, 2:63.

7. Calvin, *Comm. Ps.* (trans. Golding, xl).

8. Calvin's integrity and conviction was in many ways consistent with his father's actions. Calvin's father openly opposed the ecclesiastical corruptions of his day. As a result, in 1531 Calvin's father died having been excommunicated by the Roman church.

his policies to a less tolerant stance with regard to Protestant moorings. Consequently, Calvin began living in exile; he would seek the safety of Basel, Switzerland.

While in exile, Calvin's intentions were to devote himself to academic pursuits such as theological writing and study. In fact, it was here in Basel (1536) that Calvin produced the first version of his *Institutes of the Christian Religion*. This early version (only 516 pages in length) was significantly more concise than its latter and final incarnation. Calvin's small systematic treatment of theology was written with the purpose of moving beyond the occasional and polemical Protestant writings of his time and into a more comprehensive doctrinal presentation for his comrades within the Reformation movement.[9] After many revisions, the *Institutes* would increase significantly in size. It would eventually come to consist of four divisions or books: Book one deals with theology proper and God's role as creator. Book two examines God's role in redemption. Book three discusses the Christian life (sanctification and the role of faith). And book four contains Calvin's ecclesiology or doctrine of the church.[10]

Calvin eventually decided to settle in Strasbourg, an established Protestant city. Such an environment would have allowed Calvin to devote his energies to theological writing. He did not perceive himself to be a missionary, pastor, or Reformation activist. Rather, Calvin saw his role as a humble man of the books. However, as a result of a military operation, the direct route to Strasbourg was closed, and Calvin was forced to take a detour through Geneva. Protestantism was new and fledgling within the city of Geneva, and the leading missionary of the Reformation there was a man named William Farel. Farel soon received news that Calvin was in Geneva for the evening on his way to Strasbourg. He seized the opportunity to implore Calvin to stay in Geneva and join the Protestant cause there.[11]

Calvin resisted these pleas citing his commitment to personal study in the peaceful setting of Strasbourg. Farel, thinking it wrong to turn away from such an urgent need, issued a much stronger call to Calvin. Calvin describes the account in the following way: "He proceeded to

---

Newman, *A Manual of Church History*, 2:203.

9. Gonzalez, *The Story of Christianity*, 2:63.

10. For a detailed discussion on the theology in the *Institutes*, see Partee, *The Theology of John Calvin*, 249.

11. Gonzalez, *The Story of Christianity*, 2:64–65.

utter an imprecation that God would curse my retirement, and the tranquility of the studies which I sought, if I should withdraw and refuse to give assistance, when the necessity was so urgent." Calvin responded by agreeing to stay. He admitted that, "I was so stricken with terror, that I desisted from the journey which I had undertaken."[12] As a result of Calvin's decision to stay in Geneva, his vision of himself as a discrete theological researcher was necessarily cast away. In only a short time, Calvin's leadership would become central in Geneva's progress toward becoming a thoroughly Protestant city.[13]

PREVAILING SENTIMENTS ON THE REFORMERS AND MISSIONS

In many respects the prevailing sentiments discussed in this section are common and are typically applied to all the Protestant Reformers (Luther, Zwingli, and Calvin alike). Because of this, some of the material here is general and not only applicable to Calvin himself. Many missiological works treat sixteenth-century Protestantism together as a single unit. Now, it is true that each of the Reformers had his own unique views; yet, there is a great deal of similarity, as it relates to missiology, among these theological giants—enough to, perhaps, warrant a combined study. Nevertheless, the author will resist lingering among these generalizations and quickly move, in the next section, to a more specific analysis of Calvin himself.

Many have often posited that the sixteenth-century Reformers (Calvin included) failed in any significant way to provide a theological catalyst for missionary endeavor.[14] For example, while acknowledging that the Reformers did have a peculiar set of historical circumstances (circumstances that were an impediment to foreign mission work), Gustav Warneck makes the following statement:

> If . . . the Reformers and their immediate disciples have no word either of sorrow or excuse that circumstances hindered their discharge of missionary duty, while they could not but see the

---

12. Calvin, *Comm. Ps.* (trans. Golding, xliii).
13. Gonzalez, *The Story of Christianity*, 2:65.
14. For an example of this line of thinking refer to Verkuyl. Interestingly, Verkuyl takes this idea, that the Protestant Reformers lacked missionary zeal, for granted. Without much explanation, he moves directly to possible reasons for the Reformers's neglect of missionary work. Verkuyl, *Contemporary Missiology*, 18–19.

Church of Rome was implementing this duty on a broad scale, this strange silence can be accounted for satisfactorily only by the fact that the recognition of the missionary obligation was itself absent.[15]

Warneck goes on to spend the majority of chapter 1 in his book citing examples and reasons for (in his thinking) the Reformers's lack of missionary zeal.

For instance, Warneck believes any attempt to reveal Luther as mission minded is a confusion of "Reformation mission" with the mission of the church in general. Warneck defines missions as the "regular sending of messengers of the Gospel to non-Christian nations, with the view of Christianizing them." Luther, then, according to this argument was only concerned about the "paganised Christian church." Now, Warneck is quick to assure his readers that the Reformation did provide a needed service to the cause of missions (through its reclaiming of gospel proclamation); yet, this service was only indirect and would not be realized until a later period in Protestant history.[16]

Also, Warneck acknowledges the many statements made by Luther affirming the universality of the gospel. However, these affirmations, argues Warneck, are never made in the context of sending actual missionaries. It is insisted, then, that Luther viewed Christianity as having already accomplished its universal mission. Luther, says Warneck, believed that the apostles had preached the gospel to the whole world and, as a result, consistently looked to the past when preaching about the duty of missions. He further explains his assertion by stating that Luther and Melanchthon denied the universal application of the Great Commission; the commandment was only operative within the era of the apostles.[17]

Some special attention is also given to Calvin in Warneck's work. For example, Calvin, it is argued, did not recognize the duty of the church in sending out missionaries. Warneck refers to Calvin in the following quote: "The Kingdom of Christ is neither to be advanced nor maintained by the industry of men . . ." Warneck concludes from this quote that any sort of "special institution" for the purpose of missionary endeavor was unnecessary in Calvin's view. He also maintains that Calvin understood

---

15. Warneck, *Outline of a History of Protestant Missions*, 9.
16. Warneck, *Outline of a History of Protestant Missions*, 10–11.
17. Warneck, *Outline of a History of Protestant Missions*, 12–13, 17.

the Christian magistracy as having the sole responsibility in expanding the Christian faith into non-Christian lands.[18]

Warneck's views regarding the Reformers's neglect for missionary industry is not novel or isolated. Rather, similar ideas are commonly espoused in other missiological and historical works. Another example of this line of thinking is found in an essay written by Justice Anderson. Anderson states very plainly that the Magisterial Reformers lacked missionary zeal. He then proceeds to list several reasons for the absence of their missionary impulse. First, the Reformers are said to have misinterpreted the Great Commission as having been fulfilled within the first century. Second, the struggles associated with the Protestant Reformation itself proved to be a great distraction from the church's missionary call. Third, the Reformers's rejection of monasticism (the missionary vehicle for the Catholic Church) did not lead to the development of a suitable Protestant missionary organization as a replacement. Fourth, it is posited that "provincial ecclesiology" was a hindrance for true missionary work. Finally, the Reformers eschatology (that they were living in the last days) contradicted any sort of long-term or long-range missionary endeavor.[19]

CALVIN'S ROLE IN MISSIONS

Is it true that Calvin himself exerted, supported, and justified no missionary effort throughout his ministry? This author would answer this question in the negative. The intention, in this section, is to show Calvin as one who did in fact take seriously the Christian duty of spreading the gospel. Now, this is, of course, not to say that Calvin's theology of missions was without fault. Nevertheless, to presume Calvin as utterly lacking any sort of missionary impulse is to fail to consider the entire body of evidence. So then, what follows is an examination of the ways in which Calvin revealed his concern for the duty of missions.

In his treatment of this subject, Alonzo Ramirez opines that missions is defined in too narrow a manner by Calvin's critics.[20] Warneck's definition (presented above) provides a suitable example of such a constricted definition. Essentially, Warneck's view is that it is only Christian evangelism in a distant and predominantly pagan geographical setting

---

18. Warneck, *Outline of a History of Protestant Missions*, 19–20.
19. Anderson, "Medieval and Renaissance Missions," 194–95.
20. Ramirez, "Missiological Perspectives of Calvin's Old Testament Interpretation," 4.

that can be understood to be missionary work. Ramirez's concern here appears legitimate and self evident. Now, Warneck (and others who hold to this narrow understanding of missions) is right to raise awareness regarding the importance of foreign missions in particular. Nevertheless, one must conclude that wherever the gospel message is proclaimed, whether that be at home or abroad, this is a missionary work at its center. Certainly, when Matthew 28 refers to "all nations" one's own nation must surely be included. So then, it is necessary that as this section proceeds the idea of missions include both gospel labors in Christianized and non-Christianized settings.

Missiological Principles

With the proper context now in place, an examination of several aspects or principles of Calvin's missiological teaching is in order. The information in this section, in many ways, relied upon two separate articles[21] as primary aids in categorizing these Calvinistic principles. This categorical grid has been employed because it provides, in this author's estimation, a broad overview of Calvin's missiology in that it addresses God's superintending role along with man's duty within that context. The principles are as follows: One must be obedient to the gospel call even in the midst of difficulty. One must depend upon God to reveal opportunities for service. One's deeds or character are essential for the Christian witness. One must ultimately look to God for the certain and victorious advance of Christ's kingdom throughout the world. One must pray for the extension of Christ's kingdom. And finally, as one endeavors to fulfill the missionary mandate, God's word must be employed. What follows below is an explanation and, in some ways, an expansion (as it relates to the source articles) of these stated principles.

Calvin acknowledged the difficulty often associated with the spreading of the gospel throughout the world. He appeals to Abraham (Gen 17:23) to illustrate his point. Abraham was commanded by God to circumcise his whole family. Calvin points to the tremendous level of commitment needed in order to fulfill God's instruction. First, one must consider the amount of physical pain that such a task would inflict—particularly in a time predating modern medicine. Furthermore, Abraham would need to explain and teach his family and servants regarding

21. Calhoun, "John Calvin," 17–26, 31; Haykin, "John Calvin's Missionary Influence," 35–39.

the importance of their obedience to God. Abraham immediately and bravely obeyed the command that was issued to him. Calvin applies these biblical principles to the missionary task of the church. Such an operation appears impossible; yet, this mandate must be taken seriously through the means of active obedience. Note Calvin in the following:

> God seems to enjoin a thing impossible to be done, when he requires his gospel to be preached every where in the whole world... For we see how great the obstinacy of nearly all men, and what numerous and powerful methods of resistance Satan employs... Yet it behoves individuals to do their duty, and not to yield to impediments...[22]

So it is observed here that Calvin believed the gospel must be preached at home and beyond regardless of the difficulty that one will undoubtedly encounter.

When dealing with the notion of evangelistic endeavor, Calvin promoted an "open door" theory. This theory (at least in part) came as a result of his reading of 1 Corinthians 16:9 and 2 Corinthians 2:12. For Calvin, an "open door" is an opportunity made available providentially by God. Paul (1 Cor 16:9) speaks of this door as being "great" and "effectual." Calvin understands the door to be "great" because many souls may be won for the cause of Christ. The door is "effectual," Calvin continues, in the sense that God himself empowers and blesses the labors of the worker.[23] Calvin would also argue that a door closed is, perhaps, an indication that "no prospect of usefulness is held out."[24] So, the missionary or the gospel worker must be sensitive and aware of opportunities or the cutting off of opportunities when endeavoring to promote the kingdom of Christ.

Another missiological principle found in Calvin's teaching is that of personal holiness. One's deeds or Christian piety, in Calvin's view, is a real and legitimate factor in the promotion of the gospel at home and throughout the world. Calvin, in his commentary on Micah, promotes the idea that bringing others to the place of salvation is greatly aided when Christian workers themselves are living a life of obedience unto God: "the faithful will be so solicitous about the salvation of their brethren that they will strenuously run themselves... It is then the right way

---

22. Calvin, *Comm. Gen.* 17.23 (trans. King, 465).
23. Calvin, *Comm. 1 Cor.* 16:9 (trans. Pringle, 73).
24. Calvin, *Comm. 2 Cor.* 2:12 (trans. Pringle, 155).

of encouraging, when we really show that we require nothing from our brethren but what we desire to do ourselves."[25] Now, for Calvin good works or Christian deeds are a necessity or an integral part of the life of a true believer. Christian believers are to set the example for onlookers. This emphasis on actual holiness implies that a Christian has been given Christ, and Christ has been given not only for justification but also for sanctification.[26] Therefore, a genuine Christian will display a life of holiness and obedience, and this life of holiness will be an effective tool in the winning of lost souls.

Calvin also had a foundational perspective or teaching regarding Christ's kingdom, namely, that it is prevailing and comprehensive in character. For Calvin, the ultimate outcome of the Christian mission was never in question. Calvin was convinced that the church must look to God for the certain victory of Christ's kingdom throughout the entire world. Observe his comments to King Francis I:

> But our doctrine must tower unvanquished above all the glory and above all the might of the world, for it is not of us, but of the living God and his Christ whom the Father has appointed to rule from sea to sea, and from the rivers even to the ends of the earth.[27]

And so, it is this missiological optimism that fuels Calvin's theology in such a way as to give it (as Michael Haykin describes it) a "genuine dynamism" and a sense of "forward movement."[28]

Now, it seems relevant here to also consider Calvin's thought on the subject of prayer and its relation to missions. For Calvin, prayer is an additional aspect of the Christian's responsibility of seeking reconciliation for lost souls unto God. Prayer is one way in which the dutiful Christian expresses to God a deep desire for the salvation of humanity. For example, Calvin reveals this conviction by ending many of his sermons on Deuteronomy by praying for the salvation or the saving grace of all the earth's nations.[29] Now, some might find it difficult to resolve Calvin's doctrine of predestination with his doctrine of prayer. Regardless, Calvin

25. Calvin, *Comm. Micah* 4:1–2 (trans. Owen, 256).
26. Calvin, "Calvin's Reply to Sadoleto," 68.
27. Calvin, *Institutes*, 1:12.
28. Haykin, "John Calvin's Missionary Influence," 36.
29. Calhoun, "John Calvin," 18–19; Haykin, "John Calvin's Missionary Influence," 38.

maintained the prayer of petition as "necessary" and "not futile."[30] In his *Institutes* Calvin explains for his readers the attributes and the needfulness for prayers of petition and prayers of thanksgiving. In doing so Calvin appeals to the apostle Paul. Notice the following:

> The reason why Paul enjoins us both to pray and to give thanks without ceasing is, of course, that he wishes all men to lift up their desires to God, with all possible constancy, at all times, in all places, and in all affairs and transactions, to expect all things from him, and give him praise for all things . . .[31]

Therefore, one may observe that to Calvin prayer is a real factor in eliciting action from God (salvific activity included).

Calvin's doctrine of prayer is, perhaps, reconciled with his doctrine of divine sovereignty when one considers his teaching on the role of the Holy Spirit. For Calvin, true prayer is guided and directed by the Spirit. Therefore, Christians engaging in genuine prayer are not acting upon human impulses; rather, it is the Holy Spirit who directs the petitions of his saints.[32] And certainly, the hearts of true Christians must and will be burdened by the knowledge of a lost and dying world. Calvin believed prayer to be one of several appropriate and obedient responses to a sober knowledge such as this.

The final missiological principle discussed in this section is Calvin's priority of God's word. It has been argued that Calvin's approval of scripture translating and his writing of biblical commentaries is evidence of his appreciation of God's word and its priority in the evangelistic task. In fact, the Word was first in precedent, according to Calvin, when Old Testament prophets spoke of God's mission being extended throughout the entire world.[33] Surely then, this desire within Calvin to make scripture accessible and understandable is an outgrowth of his vision for the expansion of Christ's kingdom. This esteem for God's Word may be further observed in Calvin's practical missionary activity— his contribution to missions in France and his apparent missionary intent with regard to Brazil.

---

30. Partee, *The Theology of John Calvin*, 236.
31. Calvin, *Institutes*, 3.20.28.
32. Partee, *The Theology of John Calvin*, 236.
33. Haykin, "John Calvin's Missionary Influence," 38–39.

Calvin's Mission to France and Beyond

Calvin knew and believed that Geneva was a strategically valuable location for the cause of Protestant missions. This knowledge was not wasted or squandered by Calvin. In fact, Calvin was burdened with a sense of stewardship with regard to the missions opportunities of this small Protestant city.[34] Eventually, under Calvin's leadership, Geneva became a full fledged center for missions training.[35] Geneva was not valuable because of its great size (its population was only approximately 20,000 during Calvin's time). Rather, Geneva was important because it was a haven for many religious refugees (mostly from France). Now, these refugees did not only find safety in Calvin's Geneva, they found an opportunity to be theologically trained and then sent out to do the work of the gospel.[36]

The school in Geneva provided training to many men from France, England, and Scotland (including John Knox). And, in many ways, this school was for Calvin a response to the pleas he had received for pastors—particularly from France. As a result, the school in Geneva was no dry academic enterprise. Instead, these men were taught with the goal of receiving a ministerial assignment upon completing their studies.[37] And indeed, many missionaries were sent back to France after receiving the necessary schooling. These ministers in training received excellent instruction from some of the most notable scholars available. Thomas Lindsay describes these ministerial students as "wise, indefatigable, fearless, ready to give their lives for the work, exhorting praise from unwilling mouths, as modest, saintly, 'with the name of Jesus ever on their lips' and His Spirit in their hearts."[38] Sending these ministers back to France was not without possible repercussion—there was substantial political and religious turbulence. Nevertheless, under Calvin's direction these opportunities (however small) were seized.[39]

---

34. Calhoun, "John Calvin," 26–27.

35. In addition to what is described in this section, there is also one example of Calvin's involvement in a mission to Brazil in 1555. Unfortunately, however, this mission proved unsuccessful. For a more detailed account regarding this Brazilian mission, see Beaver, "The Genevan Mission to Brazil," 55–73.

36. Hughes, "John Calvin," 43–44.

37. Hughes, "John Calvin," 44–45.

38. Lindsay, *A History of the Reformation*, 2:133.

39. Calhoun, "John Calvin," 27.

There were records kept of Geneva's missionary activity. The records, however, are minimal and restricted to the years 1555–1562. The names of missionaries and their assignments were recorded when circumstances allowed for relatively safe documentation. In 1562 the wars of religion began in France and such record keeping became unsafe and consequently ceased. Interestingly, between 1555 and 1562 there were eighty-eight names listed of missionaries who had been sent out for gospel labor. It is argued by Philip Hughes, however, that many more than eighty-eight missionaries were sent out during these years. For example, 1561 is thought to be the year in which most of Geneva's missionary activity took place—although the records only show twelve persons that year being sent out. This figure, though, must be considered along with other sources showing at least 142 missionaries in 1561 departing for ministry assignments.[40] Consequently, one must conclude that many more than eighty-eight persons were dispatched for ministry between 1555 and 1561 (Geneva's peak years for missionary endeavor).

It is important to note at this point that this mission to France does not seem to be the result of magisterial reform. In other words, this mission was primarily the work of the Geneva church itself.[41] This may be illustrated by observing the correspondence of the French king, Charles IX, in 1561 to the company of pastors and the city council in Geneva. Essentially, the letter expressed the king's concern that many of the disputes within his country were caused by the pastors sent out from Geneva. Now, of interest here is the fact that it was not the council that accepted the responsibility for the mission; rather, it was the company of pastors. In fact, Calvin defended the missionary activity of the church by assuring Charles IX that the sent pastors were peaceful in their intentions.[42]

So then, these common descriptions of Calvin lacking any missionary impulse are plainly incorrect. Calvin did not merely theorize about the expansion of Christ's kingdom; he responded to the opportunities placed before him with decided and deliberate missionary fervor. As a result, students of church history may look to the Reformation (at least as it concerns Calvin) as a source of missiological theory and practice.

40. Hughes, "John Calvin," 45–46.

41. This point will be important to take into consideration when this writer critiques Calvin's view of magisterial reform located in an additional section below.

42. Calhoun, "John Calvin," 28–29.

MISSIOLOGICAL CRITIQUES

As was previously mentioned, this author does not presume Calvin's missiology to be without any sort of malformation. Indeed, there are several aspects related to Calvin's doctrine that appear unsuitable for one whose convictions reside among the Baptists or other free church traditions. This section, then, intends to offer a critique of Calvin's beliefs regarding the Great Commission and magisterial reform.

Calvin and the Great Commission

Is Christ's Great Commission (Matt 28:18–20) intended for all Christians in all times? Franklin Littell has argued that such a question, now, is almost universally answered in the affirmative. And further, Littell insists that this all encompassing interpretation of the Great Commission is the result of the many labors of the various free church traditions.[43] The more direct question, however, is: Did Calvin believe the Great Commission to have been issued to the apostles alone?

To begin, it seems logical to analyze Calvin's exegetical treatment of Matthew 28:19. Calvin explains verse 19 in part by stating that the apostles "should bring *all nations* to the obedience of the faith, and next, that they should seal and ratify their doctrine by the sign of the gospel." Essentially, Calvin is arguing that Christ's commission was a commission for the apostles to labor in spreading the gospel to all nations. Therefore, this office of apostle is no "empty title," but rather, it is a "laborious office."[44] How then, Calvin argues, can the Pope, steeped in hypocrisy, claim to have received this mandate as a successor to the apostles?

Calvin continually, in his comments on this passage, applies this text's meaning only to the apostles. For instance, when further commenting on verse 19, Calvin insists that "this charge is expressly given to the apostles along with the preaching of the word . . ."[45] In his ardor against apostolic succession and his concern for order and vocation, Calvin fails to apply the Great Commission to the whole of the church. This is not to say that Calvin was unconcerned with the expansion of Christ's kingdom. Nevertheless, one must search outside of Calvin's discussion on Christ's Great Commission in order to find a mandate for evangelizing.

---

43. Littell, "Protestantism and the Great Commission," 26–27.
44. Calvin, *Comm. Matt.* 28:19 (trans. Pringle, 383).
45. Calvin, *Comm. Matt.* 28:19 (trans. Pringle, 385).

This section's thesis question (Did Calvin believe the Great Commission to have been issued to the apostles alone?) may be better answered if some clarification is sought regarding Calvin's teaching on the apostolic office—in particular whether its status is ongoing or temporary. Calvin considers the office of apostle (along with evangelists and prophets) to be "extraordinary."[46] In other words, apostles served a function at a time when the church was in its infancy. Apostles were given the command to preach the gospel to all creatures. This command was issued to them without limits. Now, Calvin recognizes that apostles or evangelists may be raised up during exceptional seasons within church history. Nonetheless, this office of apostle, as a general rule, is temporary in nature.[47]

Since the office of apostle, according to Calvin, somehow corresponds to the ongoing office of pastor,[48] it seems appropriate to determine if the mandate, given to the apostles by Christ in Matthew 28, is transferred to the modern pastor. Calvin comments quite explicitly on this matter in the following:

> To the first class belongs the office of Teacher, to the second the office of Apostle; for the Lord created the Apostles, that they might spread the gospel throughout the whole world, and he did not assign to each of them certain limits of parishes . . . In this respect there is a difference between them and Pastors . . . For the Pastor has not a commission to preach the gospel over the whole world, but to take care of the Church that has been committed to his charge.[49]

To Calvin, the Great Commission was intended for the apostolic office—an office that is temporary in nature. And furthermore, the office of pastor (which corresponds historically to the apostolic office) no longer has the boundless mandate to spread the gospel. In fact, Calvin warns his readers that to presume the burden of the Great Commission for oneself is a mistake:

> The work of an Apostle is to propagate the gospel where it had not been preached, according to that command, 'Go ye, preach the gospel to every creature.' (Mark xvi. 15.) And this is what we ought carefully to notice, lest we make a general rule of what specially belongs to the Apostolic order.[50]

---

46. Calvin, *Institutes*, 4.3.4.
47. Calvin, *Institutes*, 4.3.4.
48. Calvin, *Institutes*, 4.3.5.
49. Calvin, *Comm. 2 Cor.* 12:28 (trans. Pringle, 414–15).
50. Calvin, *Comm. Rom.* 15:20 (trans. Owen, 531).

So, Christ's command, in the Great Commission, was especially for those persons in the early church who held the office of Apostle.

Writers have interpreted Calvin differently on this issue throughout the years. For example, Thomas Coates states that Calvin "rejects the idea that the Great Commission applied only to the twelve . . ."[51] In contrast, R. E. Davis claims that Calvin "definitely limits the Great Commission to the apostles."[52] Now, much of the confusion seems to lie in the presumption that if Calvin's interpretation of the Great Commission implies that the gospel mandate was limited to the apostles, then there would be no need, so the logic goes, for the continued expansion of Christ's kingdom throughout the world. This is simply untrue. For Calvin, it was not that the gospel no longer needed to be preached; instead, it was that the open and unrestricted mandate of the Great Commission was issued to the apostles alone and not to laymen or pastors. It is true that pastors, Calvin would argue, must preach the gospel; however, this duty must be attended to within the context of their own congregation. The charge of the pastor is to tend to his own flock.

Calvin did not intend to create a doctrine that made the duty of missions obsolete. His interpretation of the Great Commission was concerned with addressing at least two perceived problems. First, Calvin (as has been previously mentioned) intended to delegitimize Rome's claim to apostolic succession.[53] Also, Calvin's treatment of the apostolic office appears to have been the fruit of his concern regarding those persons (like the Anabaptists) who wandered, preaching without vocation.[54] The Anabaptists insisted that the Great Commission was binding upon all Christians in all times.[55] For Calvin this approach to gospel preaching or ministry philosophy was irresponsible and chaotic. In a letter written to the king of Poland, Calvin states:

> I perceive it to be of high importance, that nothing should be done irregularly in the church, lest thus a loose should be given to the capricious humor of each; and because it has been distinctly

---

51. Coates, "Were the Reformers Mission-Minded," 606.
52. Davis, "The Great Commission from Calvin to Carey," 44.
53. Calhoun, "John Calvin," 23; Yarnell, "The Heart of a Baptist," 74.
54. Calhoun, "John Calvin," 23.
55. Not much time has been allotted for an explanation of the Anabaptist interpretation of the Great Commission. In the following chapter, however, there will be a more detailed discussion regarding the matter.

> enjoined us by the Spirit of God . . . that all things should be done decently, and in order . . . Thus . . . no one should rashly intrude into, nor any private person usurp the office of pastor . . .[56]

Vocation and order within the ministry was for Calvin something of great importance—without it persons would be allowed to dash "about aimlessly without an assignment,[57] rashly gathering together in one place, and forsaking their churches at pleasure."[58]

For the masses who have now been influenced by the Baptist and free church movements (as it respects missions), Calvin's handling of the Great Commission (regardless of his intentions) robs the church of a direct command from their Lord to spread the gospel to all nations. Also, another potentially negative by-product of Calvin's doctrine here is that it may unintentionally and unfortunately provide the rationale for an anti-missions theology.[59] Finally, removing the mandate of unrestricted gospel preaching from the local church leaves much of the responsibility for the expansion of Christ's kingdom to the state—something that will be shown in the next section to be a valid source of concern.

Calvin and Magisterial Reform

If the apostles were given the unrestricted task of preaching the gospel to all nations, and there is no such thing (any longer) as an apostolic office, how then is Christ's kingdom to be spread throughout the world? One significant part of this answer, for Calvin, is through the means of the state or magisterial reform. Since the pastor and the layman are to remain in their own vocation and office, and since the gospel has not been preached in every land, it is the Christian magistrate who must continue the limitless duty of expanding Christ's kingdom. In fact, Calvin expresses that it is the Christian magistrates who are the successors to the apostles; it is they who have inherited the mandate to preach the gospel to every creature.[60] Now, as has been shown, Calvin certainly did promote other means of gospel proclamation besides those carried

---

56. Calvin, *Letters of John Calvin*, 3:106.

57. Of course, the Anabaptists and others of similar thinking would have certainly considered the Lord's command in Matthew 28 to have been their assignment.

58. Calvin, *Institutes*, 4.3.7.

59. To use Calvin to develop such a theology, though, would be to take him out of context.

60. Calhoun, "John Calvin," 24.

out by the state. Nevertheless, it is the state which now possesses that boundless Commission that was first given to the Lord's apostles.

But is this an aspect of Calvin's theology that ought to be celebrated? Obviously, for most, magisterial reform is now considered a negative enterprise indeed. First, the notion of magisterial reform seems to do violence to the voluntary spirit of Christianity. This is why the Anabaptists and others among the radical reformers were labeled "neo-Donatists."[61] These radical reformers actively resisted the unholy union (in their thinking) of the church and the state along with its imposition of perceived theological correctness.

A second critique of magisterial reform (something implied in the previous comments) is that it employs the use of coercion as a means to convert. Leonard Verduin has described in his work something he refers to as the doctrine of the "two swords."[62] This doctrine is a development of the post-Constantinian church (that era in church history in which the church and the state became merged together). Essentially, it teaches that the church wields a spiritual sword while the state wields (at the behest of the church) a sword of steel. The fact that the state's sword was used as a coercive tool to ensure right theological thinking may easily be established by surveying the many historical executions of "heretics" carried out with the church's approval.[63] Now, this "two sword" theory was undoubtedly carried over into the thinking and practice of the Protestant Reformers. In fact, at least one scene from Calvin's life (the burning of Michael Servetus) provides a clear historical example of the way in which the magistrate wielded its coercive and violent sword on behalf of the church.

The account of Servetus's burning is a mournful blight upon Calvin's otherwise glorious and inspiring career. Michael Servetus, who was a member of the radical movement, began a correspondence with Calvin in the year 1546. Servetus challenged Calvin regarding his understanding on the sonship of Christ, one's entrance into Christ's kingdom, and baptism. Servetus's (sometimes unorthodox) understanding of the

---

61. Donatism was a fourth-century religious movement which greatly resisted the marriage of the church with the emperor. One can easily see why the Anabaptists were referred to as "neo-Donatists." For a more complete discussion, see Verduin, *The Reformers and Their Stepchildren*, 21–62.

62. Verduin, *The Reformers and Their Stepchildren*, 42–43.

63. Verduin, *The Reformers and Their Stepchildren*, 43.

Christian faith had also previously been made known through his book *Christianismi restitutio*. In this work, Servetus challenges several key Christian doctrines of the church in his day such as: the Trinity, original sin, paedobaptism, and justification by faith.[64]

In 1553, Servetus was imprisoned in Vienne for heresy (Calvin had supplied the written evidence needed for Servetus's incarceration). After he had escaped in the summer of that same year, Servetus was next seen (August 1553) in Geneva attending a church service conducted by Calvin. Shortly after, Servetus was arrested there in Geneva and an official charge consisting of thirty-nine theological infractions was issued. Servetus was allowed to respond in writing to each of these charges. He was apparently less than convincing and as a result was sentenced to burn at the stake in October of 1553. Calvin, along with Farel, visited Servetus the day before his execution, assuring him that his death was not the product of personal offense. They also pleaded with Servetus to recant his errant beliefs. These pleadings were unsuccessful and Michael Servetus was burned to death on October 27, 1553.[65]

An honest reading of history shows with almost certain clarity that the execution of Servetus was done with the approval of Calvin. One example that reveals Calvin's attitude here is recorded in a letter he wrote to Farel in 1546. Calvin is commenting on Servetus's expressed desire to travel to Geneva. Calvin says, regarding Servetus, that, "I am unwilling to pledge my word for his safety, for if he shall come, I shall never permit him to depart alive..."[66] Now, many have argued against vilifying Calvin for his role in this episode. One's modern religious sensibilities[67] regarding issues such as these, so the argument goes, must be tempered by an attempt to consider Calvin in his own historical context—a context in which the church and the state are united. Nonetheless, regardless of historical context, this event, and Calvin's role in it, serves as a sober reminder that theological purity must never be preserved through persecution.

---

64. Greef, *The Writings of John Calvin*, 173–74.
65. Greef, *The Writings of John Calvin*, 174–76.
66. Calvin, *Letters of John Calvin*, 2:33.
67. The modern church would likely be outraged by the notion of executing someone over matters of religion. This shift in Christian conviction is certainly an intellectual and theological victory for the Anabaptists.

Calvin did, though, even in his own historical setting, receive a fair amount of criticism regarding this execution. For example, Sebastian Castellio (it is believed) released (the same year as Servetus's death) a book criticizing Calvin entitled *Historia de morte Serveti*. Calvin responded in early 1554 with *Defensio orthodoxae de sacra Trinitate*. In this work Calvin defends the church's cooperation with the magistrate in issuing capital punishment over matters of religion. He also appeals to Augustine's support of state intervention in the case of the Donatists.[68] Very soon after Calvin's response (in March) another strong critique was anonymously published (Calvin believed it to be Martin Bellius) named *Whether Heretics are to be Liquidated*. This was a scathing rebuke of Calvin and his role in the Servetus execution; yet, it was also a very careful and composed treatment on this question of killing religious heretics. Of course, a written response was quickly prepared (*Whether Heretics Should be Punished by the Civil Ruler, Against Martin Bellius*) in which Beza (it is believed) attempts to prove exegetically that religious heretics must be disciplined by the state. Incredibly, Beza appeals to Peter and the deaths of Ananias and Sophira. Beza asks by what authority did Peter put to death these persons and insists that the appropriate answer is the state.[69] One could immediately retort, it seems, that it was not Peter but God himself who took the lives of these New Testament figures.

Over one hundred years later, Calvin's role in this affair was still being lamented. For example, Thomas Grantham ended his 1691 work, *A Dialogue between the Baptist and the Presbyterian*, with a poem addressed to Calvin. It reads as follows:

> O *Calvin*, why didst thou (like *Cain*) thy pious Brother slay, Because he could not walk with thee, in thy self-chosen Way? He did, in Sacred Baptism ('tis plain) the Truth assert: And thou, by choosing Infancy (as plain) did it pervert: To which thou needst wouldst it dispense, without one word of Truth, To stand by thee in thy defence, Whilst it with open Mouth Did stand by him whilst he did plead, Repentance and true Faith, (In Sinners all) *prerequisites,* are for that Holy *Bath*. Why didst thou slander him, and then his Books to Ashes burn, Left by his Innocence, thy Wrath should to thy shame return? But some did 'scape thy furious Flames, and he by them does speak. More Truth than thou his Enemy. But yet suppose him weak, (Tho Wise and Learned

---

68. Greef, *The Writings of John Calvin*, 176–77.
69. Verduin, *The Reformers and Their Stepchildren*, 53–54.

all must grant) must he therefore be slain? And Charitable too he was, (thou dost confess): How vain Then must thou be him to oppress? Let all thy Brood take heed, They *Reprobate* no Man (as thou) by such an horrid Deed.[70]

Grantham included this address in his writing in order to aid in the prevention of any such act being repeated in the future.

One's doctrine of missions can only be negatively affected within the context of magisterial reform. Historic Calvinism's embrace of magisterial reform frustrates the notion of personal conversion by employing coercion. And, unfortunately, despite his brilliant mind and sincere intentions, Calvin's promotion of a sacral society (the state and the church as integrated) was in fact a profound malformation of his missiology.

---

70. *Southwestern Journal of Theology* has recently provided a transcription of Grantham's 1691 work in full. Grantham, "A Dialogue between the Baptist and the Presbyterian," 213–14.

4

Doctrinal Study of Andrew Fuller

A STUDY OF ANDREW Fuller and his role in the eighteenth-century English Baptist missions movement is a fascinating undertaking. This is not only true because of Fuller's practical involvement in missions work (his role as secretary of the Baptist Missionary Society[1] and his apologetic writings) but also because of the era in which he performed these activities. Fuller lived and worked in an age of Baptist history when indiscriminate gospel preaching and other missionary activity was openly scorned by many. Also, this story is, perhaps, made even more compelling when one considers that Fuller was only twenty-seven when he had largely completed his ground breaking theological contribution, *The Gospel Worthy of all Acceptation* (henceforth referred to as *The Gospel Worthy*).[2] So, it was this young, self taught, Baptist theologian and pastor who marshaled head first into a fire storm of controversy for what he believed to be an issue of utmost importance—the duty of man to believe the gospel and the Christian's duty to call sinners to repentance. Fuller then, it may be argued, is one of the more important or landmark figures in Baptist history as it relates to the subject of missions.

This chapter intends to explore Fuller's missiology by addressing several categories relevant to this topic. First, this chapter will examine Fuller's role and involvement in the BMS. Second, since it provided a theological rationale for missions, several of the arguments within *The Gospel Worthy* will be considered and analyzed. And finally, this chapter will examine several of Fuller's other writings, as it relates to his doctrine of missions.

---

1. The Baptist Missionary Society will henceforth be referred to in its abbreviated form, BMS.

2. Morden, *Offering Christ to the World*, 51.

FULLER AND THE BMS

In October of 1792, the BMS became an official reality, and Fuller was appointed as its secretary. Fuller has been described by one scholar as a less than stellar administrator in that the society operations were conducted in an informal manner and with little organization.[3] Regardless of whether this claim is valid, no one appears to question Fuller's obvious achievements and undying commitment to the BMS.[4] Fuller diligently performed many duties and filled several roles as the society's secretary such as: administrator, defender, and pastor.

Fuller as an Administrator

One way in which Fuller performed his role as administrator is through policy making.[5] For instance, Fuller in 1806 spoke to the issue of missionaries holding office in the local churches where they were stationed. He expressed in a letter that no such office was to be held by the missionaries. Also, Fuller was always adamant regarding missionaries and their involvement in radical politics. It was often argued, by their enemies, that the missionaries's presence in India was a potential threat to the British establishment there. As a result, Fuller issued a policy against any such political involvement or engagement. One example of this policy in action may be observed in the recalling of the BMS missionary Jacob Grigg. Grigg was incarcerated for inciting unrest regarding the British government in Africa. Fuller played a key role in having Grigg dismissed from his duties and having him brought home.[6]

Another administrative duty for Fuller was his role in the selection of missionary candidates. Fuller, it appears, fulfilled this duty with great seriousness. Young recounts a correspondence to William Carey where Fuller raged against the notion of a missionary candidate whose dedica-

---

3. Clipsham, "Andrew Fuller and the Baptist Mission," 7–8.

4. Fuller's loyalty may be observed by considering that he describes his labors as sitting at his desk for "10 or 11 hours every day." Fuller to Carey, 10 January 1810, The Letters of Andrew Fuller.

5. Doyle Young argues that Fuller maintained that the mission governed itself rather than the Committee. However, he is also quick to note that Fuller, regardless of this claim, engaged in a fair amount of policy making. Young, "Andrew Fuller and the Modern Mission Movement," 19.

6. Young, "Andrew Fuller and the Modern Mission Movement," 19–20.

tion to the mission was anything less than a lifetime commitment.[7] Ernest Clipsham further fortifies the claim regarding Fuller's seriousness here by stating that Fuller "was rarely, if ever overgenerous in his estimate of a candidate."[8] One example of Fuller's serious scrutiny, as it relates to missionary candidates, is seen in one of his letters to Carey in 1797. Fuller laments his inability to fulfill Carey's request for more missionaries. His main concern, in this instance, is focused upon a particular candidate's family. Fuller concludes that Bro. Reed is unsuitable for the mission field because of the "unwillingness of his wife."[9] Essentially, Fuller believed that to send inadequate missionaries into the field would do great violence to the mission as a whole. Note Fuller in the following:

> It is not for want of money that we cannot send out more missionaries, but of suitable characters. That is a matter of great importance. A Wesleyan mission to the Tronlaks in Africa has failed this last year owing to this. When they came to meet difficulties they refused to go any farther. We had better wait than send unsuitable persons.[10]

Fuller played a vital role in selecting suitable missionary candidates and, thus, doing all in his power to secure a successful foreign missionary program.

The last of Fuller's administrative duties discussed here is his role as fundraiser for the BMS. It is important when considering Fuller's fundraising activity to remember that he was not only the administrator for the BMS, he was also a full time pastor and father and husband. Yet, even with all these many obligations, history regards Fuller as having been devoted and successful in his fund raising endeavors. Clipsham attributes Fuller's success in this arena to his keen business sense and his acute awareness of personal spirituality.[11] Fuller's spiritual maturity allowed him to commit his labors to God, trusting the Lord to bless the work.

Fuller's devotion and work ethic serves as a testimony to modern ministries. Fuller travelled many hard miles for the BMS. His fund rais-

---

7. Young, "Andrew Fuller and the Modern Mission Movement," 21.
8. Clipsham, "Andrew Fuller and the Baptist Mission," 10.
9. Fuller to Carey, 6 September 1797, The Letters of Andrew Fuller.
10. Fuller to Carey, 9 August 1796, The Letters of Andrew Fuller.
11. Clipsham draws this conclusion based on a quote that Fuller made regarding the connection between the need for money in ministry and faith. Clipsham, "Andrew Fuller and the Baptist Mission," 9.

ing trips provided the occasion for Fuller to visit most all the English countries. In fact, he was absent from home and church for at least three months of every year on account of these trips.[12] Fuller's third tour of Scotland in 1805 provides an adequate illustration of his self-sacrificing commitment and his success as a fundraiser. In less than sixty days, Fuller traveled thirteen hundred miles and preached fifty sermons for the cause of missions. This tour resulted in the collection of thirteen hundred pounds, which fulfilled Fuller's goal of collecting a pound for every mile traveled.[13]

Fuller as a Theologian and Defender

Not only was Fuller a committed administrator for the BMS, he was also, perhaps, the most capable theologian and defender for the young missionary society as well. Fuller, as has been mentioned, proved his theological usefulness, in one sense, through his writing of *The Gospel Worthy*. This treatise provided the theological infrastructure needed for the cause of missions in Fuller's era (a more detailed discussion on this work will be provided later in this chapter). Yet, Fuller made an even more practical theological contribution through many of his personal letters to missionaries in the field. For example, Fuller advised the missionaries to proceed carefully in their renouncing of the caste system in India—the Lord's Supper was not to be withheld from new converts on account of this issue. On another occasion, Fuller insisted on baptizing converts who had been dipped as infants. Fuller saw no room for compromise here and made his views known to Carey without ambiguity.[14] And yet again, Fuller spoke to the issue of baptism in response to the "brethren of Serampore" and their stance against baptizing certain converts. Fuller claims, regarding this issue, that "it seems too much to neglect any part of the revealed will of Christ in complaisance to any man."[15]

Fuller's apologetic skills were also much needed throughout his years of service to the BMS. His ability to engage important officials in word and in print regarding the mission's validity proved invaluable. In

---

12. Morden, *Offering Christ to the World*, 147.
13. Young, "Andrew Fuller and the Modern Mission Movement," 26.
14. Young, "Andrew Fuller and the Modern Mission Movement," 20.
15. Fuller to Carey, 10 January 1810, The Letters of Andrew Fuller.

this way, Fuller was a great defender for the cause of missions and, in particular, the BMS throughout his lifetime. For much of its early years, the young missionary society operated without the approval of the East India Company. For this reason, Clipsham claims that if it were not "for Fuller's efforts, the Baptist mission in India might as well have been to a standstill."[16]

Relationships with important and sympathetic evangelical officials, such as William Wilberforce and Charles Grant, aided Fuller as he defended the society throughout his tenure as secretary.[17] One such occasion came in 1807 when certain critics of the mission began to circulate the notion that the missionaries's involvement with religious matters in India was an endangerment to law and civil peace there. These critics appealed to the Velore uprising[18] in 1806 as an example of their concern. Fuller, utilizing his diplomatic connections, spoke personally with many influential persons and interested parties (including the president of the Board of Control) regarding the peaceful role of the missionaries.[19]

Troubles for the society were further intensified when a pamphlet was printed by the Serampore press in 1807. The *Persian Pamphlet* (as it came to be known) was an anti-Islam writing that used severe and immoderate language in an attempt to propagate Christianity. Apparently, the pamphlet's contents were not thoroughly read prior to printing, and by the time Carey became aware of its harsh content (he quickly pulled the tract out of circulation), the damage was already done.[20] Shortly after this event, Richard Twining and John Scott-Waring began to argue, in England, in favor of Hinduism's tolerant nature in contrast to Christianity's intolerance. These arguments, which were promulgated through a series of pamphlets, were a direct attack on the Baptist mission. Others, such as William Barrow, argued that missionary work should be allowed but only by the Church of England itself. Fuller responded to this occasion by writing his *Apology for the Late Christian Missions to*

---

16. Clipsham, "Andrew Fuller and the Baptist Mission," 11–12.

17. Clipsham, "Andrew Fuller and the Baptist Mission," 12.

18. This event was a mutiny among troops from the East India Company. Since this mutiny was perceived by some to be the result of the Baptist missionaries's influence, they were forced to operate under very strict conditions for a period of time. For more information, see Morden, "Andrew Fuller as an Apologist," 247–249.

19. Clipsham, "Andrew Fuller and the Baptist Mission," 12–13.

20. Morden, *Offering Christ to the World*, 141.

India. In this work, Fuller was able to argue that the Baptist mission did not promote avarice toward the British government among its converts. In fact, the BMS actually encouraged loyalty to Britain by refusing its workers the ability to engage or interfere with politics.[21] And the fact that Fuller had always been consistent regarding the society's policy toward radical politics must have been further aid in calming concerns over political disloyalty.[22]

The time eventually came, during the East India Company's charter renewal in 1813, when Fuller and his colleagues were able to maneuver in a more proactive way as it related to the society's future security. Fuller helped secure the collection of approximately nine hundred petitions promoting a toleration clause for missionary work to be included in the East India Company's renewed charter. Wilberforce and Lord Wellesley argued on behalf of Fuller and the missionaries, and, as a result, official permission for missionary endeavor was granted and incorporated into the charter. Clipsham interprets these events in the following quote:

> The result was a triumph for Andrew Fuller in particular, who had, more than any other individual, spent himself in the struggle. At the time he was a sick man, increasingly conscious of advancing years and the strain of his labors on behalf of the Baptist Mission. He may, in a real sense, be said to have purchased the new charter with his life.[23]

So then, Fuller's commitment to instruct and defend the BMS can be observed to have been faithfully and selflessly enacted throughout his years of service as secretary.

Fuller as a Pastor

Fuller was a Baptist pastor in Kettering for many years. But, as Young rightly reveals,[24] Fuller, as the secretary for the BMS, also often fulfilled the role of pastor to his men in the mission field. In a letter he wrote to Carey in 1803, Fuller admits to and laments over his occasional lack of spiritual vibrancy. He also acknowledges Carey as having expressed

21. Clipsham, "Andrew Fuller and the Baptist Mission," 13.

22. Brian Stanley speaks about Fuller's consistent stance against political involvement on the part of missionaries, see Stanley, *The History of the Baptist Missionary Society*, 23.

23. Clipsham, "Andrew Fuller and the Baptist Mission," 14.

24. Young, "Andrew Fuller and the Modern Mission Movement," 24–26.

a sense of spiritual discouragement as well. Fuller reaches out to his brother in Christ as his pastor. Note the following:

> Let us . . . pray for each other, & strengthen each other's hands in the Lord. It is wonderful that God should do anything by such groveling sinners as we are. . . God has honoured us not a little by employing us in this great work: but as the honour does not belong to us, we must return it. The crowns do not seem to fit our heads; therefore they must be cast at the feet of Jesus.[25]

Not only does he take the time to comfort and encourage his brother, but Fuller also relates to Carey with a real sense of spiritual humility.

On another occasion, Fuller writes to his missionaries expressing his love along with other pastoral sentiments. And here also, Fuller integrates his pastoral advice, encouragements, and rebukes along with an acknowledgment of his own human frailty. Fuller states that "I am a dull flint, you must strike me agt a steel to produce fire."[26] This sort of humility mixed with firm determination is what made Andrew Fuller a good pastor and a good secretary for the BMS.

FULLER AND *THE GOSPEL WORTHY OF ALL ACCEPTATION*

A brief sketch of the main themes argued by Fuller in *The Gospel Worthy*[27] is a necessary inclusion here as an acknowledgement of the book's profound impact upon missionary activity in eighteenth-century Baptist life. As has been stated, Fuller's thesis in *The Gospel Worthy* contributed to the empowerment of his evangelical peers, namely, by providing a theological rationale for indiscriminate gospel proclamation. So, as a result, what follows below is an explanation of parts one and two of Fuller's historic treatise.[28]

One important introductory note here is that Fuller's orientation in the writing of his treatise was from the perspective of a true Biblicist. Fuller's aim appears to be focused on obedience to the Word of God.

---

25. Fuller to Carey, 6 August 1803, The Letters of Andrew Fuller.

26. Fuller to Carey, 18 April 1799, The Letters of Andrew Fuller.

27. *The Gospel Worthy* consists of a preface, three main parts, a section of concluding thoughts, and an appendix.

28. Parts one and two of *The Gospel Worthy* contain the positive arguments for Fuller's thesis. As a result of this study's nature and constraints, only parts one and two of Fuller's work will be discussed at any length.

For instance, Fuller maintains that one must embrace the whole of Scripture without neglecting those passages that appear to violate one's own theological system. Fuller argues this point in *The Gospel Worthy* as he answered those objections related to man's duty to believe the gospel in light of the Divine decrees. Notice the following:

> If I find two doctrines affirmed or implied in the Scriptures, which, to my feeble understanding, may seem to clash, I ought not to embrace the one and to reject the other because of their supposed inconsistency . . . The truth is, there is but two ways for us to take: one is for us to reject them *both*, and the Bible with them, on account of their inconsistencies; the other is to embrace them both, concluding that, as they are both revealed in the Scriptures, they are both true, and both consistent, and that it is owing to the darkness of our understandings that they do not appear to us.[29]

So then, in *The Gospel Worthy*, one could suppose that Fuller was more concerned with presenting the truth from Scripture than protecting his own theological heritage.

Fuller sets out in part one of his work to show the importance of the notion that sinners are duty bound to believe the gospel. In order to accomplish this, Fuller must define for his readers the nature of true faith. This was of great importance in Fuller's historical context. Fuller himself (with his high or hyper-Calvinistic upbringing) believed the "warrant of faith" doctrine to have devastating affects upon evangelism. This teaching, which was quite prevalent in Fuller's day, maintains that true repentance can not be realized until a person recognizes some sort of internal indication of divine election. As a result, persons under such a teaching (Fuller, for example) were likely to linger in a pre-salvific state without any sort of affirmation or assurance of salvation. This doctrine impacts evangelistic preaching because without a "warrant of faith," one can not be expected to repent. As a result, those who held to this teaching thought it improper to call for sinners to perform a deed (repentance) which they had no ability to accomplish.[30]

Fuller's first section, then, sets out to disprove that faith "consists in a persuasion of our interest in Christ." In other words, the appropriate object

---

29. Fuller, *A Gospel Worthy*, Works 2:367.

30. For a discussion on the subject of a "warrant of faith" and its relation to Fuller, see Oliver, "Andrew Fuller and Abraham Booth," 204–209.

of faith cannot be made up of something inward and subjective (a belief in one's own interest in Christ, for example). Fuller continues by arguing that such a conclusion regarding faith implies that it cannot be the duty of the unregenerate to believe the gospel, since "they are not interested in Christ, and it cannot possibly be their duty to believe a lie." But, the proper focus of faith, maintains Fuller, is not inward and subjective; rather, it is outward and objective; it is nothing short of the "glorious gospel of the ever-blessed God." And, consequently, since God has most definitely revealed his gospel to the world, one must necessarily conclude that it is the duty of humankind to believe the gospel of Christ.[31]

Fuller gives his readers four reasons for rejecting this subjective brand of faith. First, he insists that nothing can be a proper object of faith unless it has been revealed in Scripture.[32] Nowhere does God's Word speak of an inward "warrant" as being the point at which one's faith must be fixed. Scripture does, however, consistently speak of faith, Fuller continues, as having its focus set upon something from without, namely, Christ and his gospel. Also, to set the object of one's faith upon anything other than the "glory of Christ" is to prove one's faith to be of the vain sort and to find oneself yet in sin. Finally, Fuller maintains that the many New Testament examples of faith being exercised (healing accounts and so on) are shown to be focused upon the "all-sufficiency" of Christ.[33] Consequently, saving faith does not terminate upon any sort of inward inclination or perceived interest in Christ; instead, when the gospel is proclaimed to sinners, one must only look to Christ (Fuller would argue) and believe.

Section two sets out to prove that it is surely the duty of all men who hear the gospel to respond in faith. Fuller accomplishes this task by putting forth six separate arguments. First, faith in Christ is man's duty because Scripture openly and consistently commands lost humanity to believe.[34] Fuller illustrates this point by appealing to a lengthy list of Scriptural proofs. One example is seen in Fuller's handling of John 6:27–29. The persons addressed by Jesus here, argues Fuller, were not true believers. They are being rebuked by Christ for following after him solely because their physical hunger had been satisfied. Beginning in verse 27, Jesus

---

31. Fuller, *A Gospel Worthy*, Works 2:333.

32. This is another example of Fuller as an ardent Biblicist. His criteria does not allow for a speculative theology here.

33. Fuller, *A Gospel Worthy*, Works 2:334–35.

34. Fuller, *A Gospel Worthy*, Works 2:343.

reprimands these unbelievers and implores them to not labor after those things that perish; rather, they must seek after eternal life.[35] And in verse 29, the audience is exhorted with the following: "Jesus himself answered and said, 'this is the work of God, that you have faith in the one whom he sent'"[36] Fuller insists that Christ's command in this text encapsulates the "first and greatest of all duties."[37] Unbelieving mankind is implored in this passage to believe in Christ, the one whom God has sent.

Fuller's second argument maintains that mankind is bound to embrace whatsoever God reveals.[38] Fuller is making a very simple deduction at this point. If God commands humankind to have faith in Christ, then an appropriate response to such a revelation must surely be considered a duty for those who hear. If faith or belief in God's revelation, Fuller continues, is not a duty, then mankind cannot be regarded as under the curse of sin. It is no sin to ignore that which carries with it no sense of obligation.[39] Of course, the obvious implication is that lost humanity is under a moral obligation to respond to whatsoever God reveals—Christ being chief among God's revelation.

In his third argument, Fuller asserts that "though the gospel, strictly speaking, is not a law, but a message of pure grace; yet it virtually requires obedience, and such an obedience as includes saving faith."[40] Essentially, Fuller maintains that while the Gospel (which represents the goodness of God) may not be considered a law, in a formal sense, it certainly deserves a profound response of gratitude. Fuller continues by stating that the gospel "is the greatest overflow of Divine goodness that was ever witnessed. A return suitable to its nature is required *virtually* by the gospel itself, and *formally* by the Divine precept on its behalf." As a result, it is deemed offensive to presume that God's gracious offer to mankind warrants only an audience and not obedience.[41]

---

35. Interestingly, Fuller refers to John 6:27 in another instance where he seems to guard its interpretation, perhaps indirectly, from the doctrine of preparation: "It is a grievous misapplication . . . to consider it as expressive of a mere attendance upon the means of grace, without any spiritual desire after God; and to allow that unregenerate sinners comply with it." Fuller, *A Gospel Worthy*, Works 2:347.

36. Author's translation.

37. Fuller, *A Gospel Worthy*, Works 2:345.

38. Fuller, *A Gospel Worthy*, Works 2:349.

39. Fuller, *A Gospel Worthy*, Works 2:349–50.

40. Fuller, *A Gospel Worthy*, Works 2:352.

41. Fuller, *A Gospel Worthy*, Works 2:352–53.

Fuller proceeds with his fourth point by depicting man's want of faith as a product of willful and moral depravity. At this point Fuller begins to make a distinction between natural and moral inability.[42] To argue, according to Fuller, that sinners are not obliged to believe the gospel on account of inability or their being dead in sin (without distinguishing between natural and moral inability) is without warrant. How can one be condemned as sinful for neglecting that which is naturally impossible? It must be concluded, then, that Scriptural calls for faith in Christ demand obedience and are within the realm of humankind's natural ability, and the sinful rejection of such calls may be properly understood to be the result of moral inability.[43]

The fifth argument made by Fuller speaks to God's punishment as it pertains to unbelief. Fuller, while employing several Biblical passages, essentially maintains that God warns lost humanity of the dire repercussions associated with not believing on the Lord Jesus. He further argues that "it is . . . taken for granted that nothing but sin can be the cause of God's inflicting punishment, and nothing can be sin which is not a breech of duty." And so, this awesome and sober warning, which is enshrined in the Great Commission, has been entrusted to God's people. The Commission is a message of hope, and yet, it is also a message of damnation to those who do not believe. And a warning of impending punishment surely implies the necessity of duty and obligation.[44]

Fuller's last argument in part two of his book posits that "other spiritual exercises, which sustain an inseparable connexion with faith in Christ, are represented as the duty of men in general." Fuller insists that a spiritual blessing is the result of a proper response to a spiritual exercise. Love for God, which is a spiritual exercise, is expressed through thankfulness and an appreciation for God's glorious character. So too is love for Christ to be considered a spiritual exercise. Those who love Christ are promised a spiritual blessing, namely, favor with God. Yet, to those who hear the gospel, love for Christ is also a duty. Fuller reveals this truth by appealing to Paul in his condemnation of those who "love not our Lord Jesus." The passivity on the part of the sinner here in not

---

42. For more details on Fuller's adoption of the Edwardsian distinction between natural and moral inability, see Chun, "A Mainspring of Missionary Thought."

43. Fuller, *A Gospel Worthy*, Works 2:354–55.

44. Fuller, *A Gospel Worthy*, Works 2:358.

loving Christ reaps the same woeful outcome as those who would hate Christ with positive volition.[45]

The Gospel Worthy was at its heart a missionary document. Clipsham claims that the purpose of Fuller's work here was to "remind the Church of its missionary task."[46] The theological rationale that *The Gospel Worthy* provided for open and indiscriminate evangelism was not received without controversy. Nonetheless, Fuller's message was another important advance upon hyper-Calvinism and its estrangement from evangelistic proclamation.

MISSIOLOGICAL PRINCIPLES

As has been shown, Fuller was a man who took serious the missionary mandate of the church. In addition to his practical work as secretary for the BMS, Fuller also spend much of his energy convincing his listeners and readers of the great importance of fulfilling Christ's command to spread the gospel. This section intends to gather and analyze several prominent missiological principles found within a selection of Fuller's published writings.

The Urgent Call

For Fuller, it is a terrible sin to know that Christ has commissioned his church to propagate the message of the gospel and yet delay. This principle is evident in a sermon Fuller preached at Clipstone in 1791, entitled *Instances, Evil, and Tendency of Delay, In the Concerns of Religion* (henceforth referred to as *Delay, In the Concerns of Religion*).[47] In this sermon Fuller makes use of Haggai 1:2. This passage portrays the formally exiled Israelites as procrastinating in their rebuilding of the Lord's temple. The people did not doubt the need for such a task; rather, they simply consoled their slothful delay by rehearsing the following sentiment: "the time is not come." Fuller takes this text and applies it to several examples related to religious duties in his day, including the work of missions.[48]

45. Fuller, *A Gospel Worthy*, Works 2:360–63.

46. Clipsham, "Andrew Fuller and Fullerism," 214.

47. This sermon was preached at a minister's conference held at Clipstone in April of 1791. The preaching of this sermon is commonly held up as one of the important factors leading to the formation of the BMS. For additional discussion concerning this sermon, see Morden, *Offering Christ to the World*, 130–33.

48. Fuller, *Delay, In the Concerns of Religion*, Works 1:145–51.

In light of the Great Commission, Fuller laments over the weak and infrequent missionary efforts made by the church of his day.[49] Essentially, Fuller pronounces that such a lack of urgency is evil and disobedient at its core. For example, to procrastinate in this way is to ignore the many Scriptural commands in which persons are "required to attend to Divine things immediately." Fuller illustrates his point with a narrative describing a company of men who break from their work for a time of rest. There is a moment in which impending danger comes upon these men and all but one is awakened. The sleeping worker cannot be roused despite the efforts of his comrades, and, as a result, he is lost. Fuller describes the deep sense of regret one would feel over such a scenario. He also contrasts this sorrow with the more acute pain that is associated with a lost soul. After illustrating his point with great clarity, Fuller soberly implores his audience to action: "My dear hearers! Consider your condition without delay. God says to you, *Today*, if ye will hear his voice, harden not your hearts."[50] So then, urgency, with regard to the missionary mandate of the church, was a noticeable characteristic in Fuller's theology.

Human Means

Though he never neglected the sovereignty of God as foundational to the missionary task, Fuller, nevertheless, stressed human endeavor as the ordinary means by which lost humanity is reconciled unto God. Fuller argued this point in defense against those who insisted that the Baptist missionaries were unnecessary because the Hindus could not be converted by human labors. In the following, Fuller's response reveals his strong conviction regarding human responsibility and the missionary mandate: "We perfectly agree with our opponents that the Hindoos can never be converted by mere *human means*, though we are equally persuaded that they will never be converted without them."[51] This line of thinking (in his *Delay, In the Concerns of Religion*) may also be detected in Fuller's rejection of those persons who simply pray for lost souls without laboring for them. Why should one expect prayers for salvation to be answered outside of the context of human endeavor? The apostles and

---

49. Fuller, *Delay, In the Concerns of Religion*, Works 1:147.
50. Fuller, *Delay, In the Concerns of Religion*, Works 1:150–51.
51. Fuller, *Apology*, Works 2:821.

the early church certainly engaged in the proclamation of God's word as the primary means for directing lost souls unto God. Consequently, Fuller insisted that the conversion of mankind would never take place without evangelistic preaching.[52]

For Fuller, the evangelistic task of the church was an issue in which love for the Creator and humanity hung in the balance. Fuller rejected any notion that allowed contentment at the expense of lost humanity. With respect to this attitude, Fuller maintains that "such a spirit, though complimented by some as liberal, is mean, and inconsistent with the love of either God or man."[53] Human means, then, is to be carried out with a sense of true devotion. To withhold such endeavors is to withhold one's love for God and man.

Moral character was another concern for Fuller as it related to human endeavor and the missionary task. Fuller insisted that the missionaries avoid the distractions of seeking wealth and power. They must rather focus their attention on the conversion of lost souls, seeking to employ only those means that are appropriate and befitting of a Christian missionary such as: gospel proclamation, persuasive discourse, teaching, and Bible distribution. These ordained means, however, can only suffer violence if the moral character of missionary workers is found to be in want. Fuller warned his co-laborers that the un-Christian world would judge God and the Christian religion based on the merits of one's own moral behavior. For this reason, the Christian evangelist or missionary must diligently work to ensure that Christ is not portrayed in an incorrect manner as a result of immoral conduct.[54]

The Final Triumph of Christ

Another missiological distinctive to be found in Fuller is his eschatological optimism. Clipsham claims that Fuller "had no doubts as to the ultimate success of the gospel, whatever the difficulties, setbacks and disappointments might have to be experienced first." The positive nature of Fuller's missionary drive was the result, in part, of his eschatological convictions. Fuller believed that in order for the peace that is characteristic to the

---

52. Fuller, *Delay, In the Concerns of Religion*, Works 1:147–48.

53. Fuller, *Apology*, Works 2:818.

54. Clipsham, "Andrew Fuller and the Baptist Mission," 7; Morden, *Offering Christ to the World*, 138.

Millennium to be realized, the great battle (which will surely end in victory) must be waged through the obedient efforts of the church.[55]

And so, Fuller worked diligently with this sanguine attitude. He, of course, believed that the sure victory of Christ throughout the world was a Biblical concept. Notice Fuller in the following:

> If we believe the Scriptures, (and if we do not we are not Christians,) we must believe that all nations are promised to the Messiah *for his inheritance*, no less than the land of Canaan was promised to the seed of Abraham; and we, as well as they, ought, in the use of those means which he has appointed, to go up and endeavor to possess them.[56]

Ultimately, Fuller's missiological comfort rested in his belief that Christ's presence would be ever with the labors of his Church: "Our hope arises from the hope of Christ to be with his servants in the execution of their mission to the end of the world."[57]

The Great Commission

Michael Haykin rightly argues that Matthew 28:19–20 had, historically, been a key ecclesiological text for the English Baptists in their development of the doctrine of believer's baptism. However, it was Fuller along with several of his peers (William Carey, for example) that began to stress again the missiological focus of this epic text.[58] As has been discussed in the previous chapter, it was not uncommon for Reformed theologians to interpret the Great Commission within the context of the Apostles alone—failing to apply the Commission's mandate to the modern church. This errant approach (as will be displayed further in this section) found no sympathy among Fuller and his comrades as they fought to reestablish the vibrant missiological focus of the Baptist denomination.

Fuller's comprehensive interpretation of the Great Commission was certainly not a historical anomaly. The Anabaptists, for example, understood this text to be binding upon all Christians in all times. Franklin Littell makes this argument and supports it by appealing to the fact that

---

55. Fuller expresses his thoughts in a letter (quoted by Clipsham) on the church's missionary role leading up to the millennium, see Clipsham, "Andrew Fuller and the Baptist Mission," 7.

56. Fuller, *Apology*, Works 2:818.

57. Fuller, *Apology*, Works 2:821.

58. Haykin, "Andrew Fuller on Mission: Text and Passion," 27–28.

the Anabaptists made continual use of the Great Commission as a proof text in sermons as well as apologetic writings.[59] For instance, Menno Simons claims that to "preach the Word correctly and beneficially is the highest and greatest command enjoined upon a preacher by Christ, even as He said, Go ye into all the world, and preach the gospel to every creature."[60] Littell further claims that the "Anabaptists were among the first to make the Commission binding upon all church members." As a result, these restitutionist Christians can rightly be called "forerunners of the modern missionary movement."[61]

Fuller was without a doubt in harmony with the Anabaptists regarding the right application of the Great Commission to all Christians in all times. For Fuller also, this theme of obedience to Christ's Commission was common in his works. In his famous sermon, *Delay, in the Concerns of Religion*, Fuller scolds his audience for their lack of missionary action (among other things). He points to the apostles and their tireless efforts for the sake of the gospel as an example to the modern Christian. Christ commanded them to go and preach to every creature. The apostles pursued their Lord's command without regard for difficulty or persecution. Yet, the commission issued to the apostles is also the modern Christian's commission. Fuller laments that "since their days, we seem to sit down half contented that the greater part of the world should still remain in ignorance and idolatry."[62]

In *The Gospel Worthy* Fuller uses the Great Commission (as recorded in Mark) as a proof that faith is the duty of all who hear the gospel. The Apostles were to preach the message of Christ to all persons. If this message is rejected, then the result can only be condemnation. Fuller argues that such a warning of condemnation demands the conclusion that it is the duty of all who hear to believe. He further claims that it "is as if our Lord had said, This is your message . . . go and proclaim it to all the nations . . ."[63] Therefore, sinners are duty bound to believe the gospel, and Christians are, likewise, duty bound to preach the gospel.

Fuller's understanding of the Great Commission may also be observed in his *Apology for the Late Christian Missions to India*. There is a

---

59. Littell, "The Anabaptist Theology of Missions," 12.
60. Simons, *The Foundation of Christian Doctrine*, Works 164.
61. Littell, *The Anabaptist View of the Church*, 112–13.
62. Fuller, *Delay, In the Concerns of Religion*, Works 1:147.
63. Fuller, *The Gospel Worthy*, Works 2:358.

particular section where Fuller explains the basis for the Baptists's missionary activity in India. He claims that their efforts are not the result of "misguided zeal." Rather, they are committed to the will of God as it is revealed in Scripture. Fuller asserts that if their efforts are not authorized by the New Testament, then they are without any true authority. Fuller maintains the following:

> We have no notion of any thing being the will of God, but what may be proved from the scriptures . . . The principle ground on which we act is confined to a narrow compass: it is the commission of our Saviour to his disciples, "Go—teach all nations;" which commission we do not consider as confined to the apostles, because his promised presence to them who should execute it extends "to the end of the world."[64]

So, one of Fullerism's foundational missiological principles is its ardent belief in the Great Commission as binding upon all Christians. Christ has commanded his Church to go and proclaim the gospel, and go it must.

Fuller's missiology is a devoutly Biblical and optimistic theology in which lost humanity is brought to faith as a result of God-ordained human endeavor. Fuller was deeply moved by a sense of missionary obligation, which was, for him, obedience to God's word. He recognized this duty for missionary labor (which was encapsulated in the Great Commission) and sought with great urgency to implore his fellow Baptists to recognize it as well. Fuller sought to obey Christ's missionary call in a very practical way by serving as the secretary for the BMS. Yet also, Fuller endeavored to promote the church's missionary mandate through his sermons and apologetic writings. And so it was that Fuller lived to see hyper-Calvinism's gross neglect for indiscriminate evangelistic preaching largely fade into the background. The time was right for the success of Fullerism. Clipsham claims that "it was Fuller's distinction that . . . demolished the foundations of false Calvinism . . . *Fuller provided a theology such as thinking men were seeking.*"[65]

---

64. Fuller, *Apology*, Works 2:817.
65. Clipsham, "Andrew Fuller and Fullerism," 269.

5

Conclusion

Historically and even to this day, the title "Calvinism" has often been worn comfortably by many among the Baptist tradition. For example, when Fuller was asked about the varieties of Calvinistic perspectives among his peers, he detailed three separate strands: high, moderate, and strict Calvinism. Fuller considered high Calvinism to be well outside the bounds of Calvin's teaching—approaching antinomianism. Moderate Calvinism, for Fuller, was a mixture of Calvinism and Arminianism. Strict Calvinism was that strand that most closely adhered to Calvin's own teaching. Fuller, while insisting that he does not promote everything that Calvin taught, makes the assertion that: "I reckon strict Calvinism to be my own system."[1] So, for the Baptist, "Calvinism" has not been a term of derision.

Yet, Fuller, as was stated, does makes clear that he did not advocate all of Calvin's teachings. It is qualifications like this that inspire new and, sometimes, more helpful theological descriptors. What, then, are the differences between Fullerism and Calvinism? This book has sought to answer this question most particularly as it relates to missiology. This final chapter seeks to perform several concluding tasks. First, there will be a brief summary of the main points argued or detailed in this paper. Second, this chapter will then discuss those areas where Fuller and Calvin harmonize with respect to their missiology. Third, those areas of missiological disagreement will also be discussed. Last, a section of final remarks will detail several conclusions answering the thesis question of this book as a result of the evidence presented.

---

1. Fuller, *Memoir*, Works 1:77.

SUMMARY

The term Calvinism very often is used by many to describe a soteriological system or perspective. Yet, Calvinistic doctrine bears on other theological categories such as ecclesiology and missiology. Indeed, there are aspects of Reformed doctrine that are clearly incompatible within a Baptist context. One must only consider the doctrine of infant baptism to make a conclusion such as this. As a result, a more accurate and descriptive nomenclature is needed when discussing Baptist theology. Fullerism, while admittedly associated with Calvinistic soteriology,[2] may provide a superior theological template to help preserve an emphasis of Baptist distinctives.

Andrew Fuller was a descendant of the English Particular Baptists. These devout Christians were influenced by Reformed theology, and yet, they undoubtedly made several important qualifications regarding this association. One such qualification was certainly noticeable in the development of believer's baptism—a doctrine that, for the Particular Baptists, appears to have been impacted by Menno Simons's *Foundation Book*.[3] So then, Andrew Fuller and, consequently, Fullerism maintains a theologically genetic connection to these early dissenting Baptist pioneers.

Fullerism also has made major contributions, historically, to the doctrine of missions. So, Calvin's missiology, for the objective of this comparative study, becomes important for the purpose of clarity. Calvin, regardless of caricatures to the contrary, had a genuine missiological impulse. His writings, along with the witness of history, highlight several doctrines that can be considered together as a body of missiological principles. They are as follows: Obedience to the gospel call, even when difficult, is obligatory. God will reveal opportunities for gospel service. One's moral conduct is fundamental for the Christian witness. The victorious advance of Christ's kingdom throughout the world is certain. Prayer, as a missionary tool, is needful for the expansion of Christ's kingdom. And finally, the use of God's Word is essential when endeavoring to fulfill the missionary mandate.

---

2. For now, Fuller's own stated commitment to a Calvinistic soteriology will suffice in validating this claim. A more thorough investigation of Fuller's soteriology and its potentially unique emphasis, as it respects Calvinism, must be postponed for a future project.

3. See chapter 2 for a review of the details for this assertion.

Now, Calvin's perspective regarding the Great Commission is something that falls outside the bounds for not only the Anabaptist tradition but also for the Baptist tradition (at least as it regards Fuller and future Baptist generations). Calvin, in an attempt to discredit apostolic succession and the wonderings of the Anabaptists, did not transfer that boundless comprehensive missionary mandate contained in the Great Commission to future non-apostolic generations of Christians. Also, Calvin was a Magisterial Reformer. In other words, for Calvin, it was proper for the church and the state to be united in a certain sense. The result of this marriage was that the state, at the behest of the church, sometimes used means of coercion in order to achieve a standard of right belief. The execution of Michael Servetus serves as an adequate example of Calvin and his involvement in the magisterial model.

Conceptually, Fuller made a significant contribution to the historic cause of missions. For instance, he helped lay the theological infrastructure needed for the missionary impulse to be revived in his era through the writing of *The Gospel Worthy*. Fuller also stressed other issues related to missions such as: The gospel call demands an urgent response. The conversion of souls takes place through the ordinary means of human endeavor. Christ's triumph throughout the world is a certainty. Finally, the Great Commission, for Fuller, was a call intended for all Christians in all times.

POINTS OF AGREEMENT

There are several points of agreement between Calvin and Fuller as it regards the missiological principles discussed here in this book. Undoubtedly there are other missiological commonalities between these two theologians than those which are listed here; however, this chapter will restrict itself to detailing only those correlations that are most noticeable between chapters 3 and 4. One example of agreement is the belief that Christ's kingdom will undoubtedly triumph throughout the entire world. Both Calvin and Fuller, in this respect, maintained a great eschatological optimism. The missionary work of the church, according to Calvin and Fuller, was leading to a profound and comprehensive embrace of Christ by all the world's nations. There is, though, a fundamental difference between Calvin and Fuller as it relates to the methodology of this triumphal spread of Christ's kingdom. This difference, however, will be detailed below in the following section. This author could spend a great deal of time discussing issues related to post-millennial theology. However, while being aware of the implications of an evolution of eschatological thought, such a discussion is outside the scope of this paper.

Moral conduct is also a recognizable correlation between Calvin and Fuller as it relates to their missiologies. Moral character, for Calvin, was a tool for one who is seeking to promote the cause of Christ. The Christian worker or missionary must prove that what is required of those outside the faith is also required of those within the faith. Fuller's thought on this subject is right in step with Calvin's view. He urged his missionaries to live holy lives because the lost world would judge their religion and their God based upon their moral behavior.

A high regard for Scripture and its role in the missionary task is a further connection between the missiologies of Calvin and Fuller. The observation of Calvin's commitment to translating and commenting upon God's word reveals, for this Reformer, the Bible's place of importance within the evangelistic task of the church. Esteem for the Scriptures is also a recognizable trait in Fuller's work. For example, when building his case for man's obligation to believe and to proclaim the gospel, Fuller appeals to Scriptural mandates. In response, for instance, to Christ's missionary mandate in Mark 16, Fuller expresses to his readers that this is "your message . . . go and proclaim it . . ."[4]

POINTS OF DISAGREEMENT

There are, however, several points of missiological disagreement between Calvin and Fuller. Clearly, as has been established, Calvin's understanding of the Great Commission is contrary to Fuller's approach. Fuller, unlike Calvin, believed that not only did the gospel call of the Great Commission transfer to all Christians in all times, but that the boundless and limitless aspect of Christ's Commission transferred to all generations as well. One can validate this claim by reading Fuller's sermons and other treatises in which the mandate of the Commission is issued and applied to the church as a whole.[5]

Another point of disagreement between Calvin and Fuller is with their approach regarding the teaching of Christ's final triumph. It is true

---

4. Fuller, *The Gospel Worthy*, Works 2:358.

5. Refer back to chapter 4 of this book for a review of Fuller's handling of the Great Commission.

(as has been shown above) that Calvin and Fuller, broadly speaking, agreed on this doctrine—that, as a result of missionary endeavor, the message of Christ will ultimately triumph in all nations. Yet, there is an aspect of disharmony here between Calvin and Fuller's methodology. For Calvin, there is an aspect of missionary endeavor which includes the magistrate. For example, the state wields the sword in order to ensure right belief.[6] Also, the state has inherited the boundless mandate to spread Christ's kingdom throughout the world.[7] Now for Fuller, Christ's final triumph was to be realized without any use of the state's coercive sword. Rather, Christ's kingdom, argues Fuller, was to be spread without any use of physical force. Fuller's missionary optimism found its source in the hope of Christ's promise "to be with his servants in the execution of their mission to the end of the world."[8] Now of course, the methodological differences between Calvin and Fuller on Christ's final triumph speaks also to the issue of magisterial reform. Calvin and Fuller, obviously, as the above information reveals, understand the role of the state and the church quite differently.

CONCLUDING REMARKS

As a result of this book's research, Fullerism, as it relates to the Baptist tradition, is deemed to be a more compatible and, consequently, a more helpful nomenclature than Calvinism. In a certain sense this conclusion is a very simple and logical deduction. For instance, Fuller maintains his Baptist heritage by adhering to the doctrine of believer's baptism. This assertion is made evident by recalling Fuller's correspondence with Carey wherein he insisted that new converts in India, even those baptized as infants, undergo believer's baptism.[9]

This book's primary focus, however, is centered upon a missiological comparison between Fullerism and Calvinism. As has been shown, these two theological perspectives find agreement on several accounts. Nevertheless, the differences between Fuller and Calvin on issues such as the Great Commission and magisterial reform are not peripheral and must be seriously considered. Fuller's comprehensive interpretation of

---

6. Calvin's role in the execution of Michael Servetus validates this claim.
7. See chapter 3 for a review of this information.
8. Fuller, *Apology*, Works 2:821.
9. Refer to chapter 3 for further discussion.

the Great Commission was one of the exegetical keys for his promotion of a revival of missionary zeal in his day—something that remains an emphasis among contemporary Baptists and, thus, is a distinctive for the denomination. This different hermeneutic between Calvin and Fuller here is important because to fail to understand Christ's limitless commission as binding upon all Christian generations is to open the door for an outright rejection of indiscriminate gospel proclamation (something that had occurred in Fuller's own context). Now, Calvin, it is true, did not reject missionary endeavor. Nonetheless, his interpretation of the Great Commission restricted gospel proclamation in that it removed, from post-apostolic generations of Christians, the boundless and unlimited mandate to spread the gospel. As a result, the duty of boundless kingdom expansion was shifted, in many ways, over to the magistrate.

Here at this point, as it regards magisterial reform, one may observe another crucial missiological distinction between Fuller and Calvin—an issue that causes one to concede that Fullerism is a superior descriptor or theological landmark for the Baptist. Fuller believed that Christ's kingdom must and will be expanded throughout the entire world. Yet, this must be accomplished solely through the work of the church and, consequently, without any sort of coercion.[10] This concern for the voluntary spirit of Christianity is certainly the prevailing sentiment of contemporary Baptists (and Evangelicalism in general), and it is Fuller along with other non-magisterial Christians that have, historically, maintained and promoted this non-coercive brand of Christian faith. When one considers, as it respects the Baptist heritage, the importance of a non-constraintive missionary focus, along with its Scriptural impetus—the Great Commission, one cannot help but conclude that Fullerism, as opposed to Calvinism, is a superior Baptist theological nomenclature.

---

10. Morden speaks to this issue. He argues that Fuller's approach to missionary work was conducted in such a way that it rejected the use of force and was consistent with free choice, see Morden, *Offering Christ to the World*, 144.

Appendix A

An Interview with Dr. James Leo Garrett, Jr.

Mauldin: In an article you wrote entitled, *How Prominent Baptists Stack Up*, which I discovered in an Alabama Baptist publication, you discussed how closely significant Baptists have adhered to Dortian Calvinism. In this article, you argued that Fuller could only be described as a two-point Calvinist, affirming limited atonement and irresistible grace. There are, of course, many who would understand Fuller as residing much closer to Dortian Calvinism than your assessment allows. In particular, Dr. Nettles in his *By His Grace and for His Glory* argues that Fuller was a thorough-going Calvinist. Michael Haykin would make a similar argument. In what way does Fuller violate a Dortian perspective with regard to total depravity, unconditional election, and perseverance of the saints?

Garrett: Well, Chad, I should say first of all that this article you're referring to is one of a series of six articles published in the *Alabama Baptist*. And, there is a larger context for this discussion, but you're right in pointing to this statement that I made about Fuller. Very soon after the article was published in 2007, Dr. Tom Ascol, the editor of *Founders Journal* (who was once my student here) wrote me at some length about these articles, and partly to show me that he was telling some of the neo-Calvinists, who were getting hot and disturbed about my articles, to kind of cool down a little bit. But, also to challenge me at the point that you have, and I immediately said to him—and that's the correspondence that I haven't been able to find—but I think I'm right in that I wrote back to him that I was certainly wrong about perseverance. I don't know why I didn't include perseverance in those. I should never have said two-point; I should have at least said three-point, because there is no question about perseverance. And so I said I would get back to him. Well, it's been all these months and I haven't gotten back to him. Maybe now after talking with you I can get back to Dr. Ascol. But, the other point I would make is that I don't subscribe to the TULIP as the most accurate way of defining the differences between the Remonstrants and the Synod of Dort—thinking, rather, that it is the nature of repentance and faith that is really that crucial issue. So that would mean that instead of talking about total depravity here, I would want to talk about repentance and faith. And I noticed that in *The Gospel Worthy of All Acceptation*—I was looking at this last night—in his [Fuller's] treatment, he very clearly talks about both given by God and the duties of man. It's very much of a both-and answer. It's answering the objections, I believe here where he discusses that. Here it is, it's on page 380 of volume two.

Mauldin: Of the Sprinkle edition?

Garrett: Yes—part of *The Gospel Worthy of All Acceptation*—he says, "The scriptures uniformly teach us that all our sufficiency to do good and abstain from evil is from above. Repentance and faith, therefore, may be duties notwithstanding their being the gifts of God." So I see him as taking almost a Calminian position on that question. He is arguing so strongly for the duty of faith that you have to see that he's stronger on that than the Synod of Dort.

Mauldin: Right, that's what he's emphasizing over and above—

Garrett: He doesn't deny the other, so I see that as a mediating position. That leaves us the question about unconditional election, and I would simply say that I need to read him more and see where I am mistaken, if I am, at that point. I think he does probably not get away from that as much as I inferred in this listing. So, you notice I don't have this statement in my book [*Baptist Theology*], if you notice that. This that you quote is not in the book under Fuller; I did not make those statements. I did in the context of—I was asked to do those articles in Alabama by the editor of the paper, because they were having churches in Alabama that were torn up over the issue of Calvinism. I was supposed to be able to pour a little oil on the waters over there, and I don't know that I did. But that was the context, and I think that I was a bit hasty. I try to be more careful, and I think that I shouldn't have made that statement. I should have qualified it more. But, I think it reduces it down to one point—it really is the question of election, and I need to go back and read some of his lesser writings and see if I can pick up on any points that I didn't have by reading his major writings.

Mauldin: Well, perhaps, by the standard that you discussed—repentance and so on, rather than total depravity—in other words, you were saying that there was an emphasis on man's duty; and, because of that emphasis, that perhaps that's a modification on traditional Dortian Calvinism. You could probably say the same thing about unconditional election, if that's the criteria that you're using.

Garrett: He's moving a little bit into *via media*, the way between the two positions, it seems to me. Of course, Dan Taylor tried to get him over to general atonement and never did succeed. So I recognized that. And I may be wrong about the election; I need to look at that. That would be my statement today. I need to go back and read him much more in detail, some of the lesser writings, to see if I can pick up evidence of what he's done there. So I would say that my statement was a little bit ill-advised, and I should have been more cautious about making that statement. But I think that on the faith and repentance area, it's a mediating position. On perseverance, I would certainly say that I was wrong there. I'll leave the other open-ended at this point.

Mauldin: Do you think that there is any sort of conflict of interest in saying, "I am Baptist, and I am Reformed," or perhaps as a Baptist, any unwanted baggage wrapped up in the designation Reformed or Calvinist. Richard Muller wrote an article called *How Many Points*, and in that he's arguing that there is a lot more to being a Calvinist than soteriology. In other words, it's part of a larger confessional heritage, and so, if a Baptist or any other person that is disconnected from that heritage says, "I am a five-point Calvinist," there's something a little bit wrong with that, according to Muller—that it's disconnected from the broader context. And so, what are your thoughts about that, Dr. Garrett?

Garrett: Well, I would say that Baptists either do not or should not buy into the whole Reformed tradition. That would be my general thesis. Baptists do not or should not—if they try to—buy into the entire Reformed tradition. Well, that ought to be obvious on an issue like infant baptism, or on the nature of the church—some of these ecclesiological issues that are the Baptist distinctives. We shouldn't have to waste any time to acknowledge that there we're not Reformed. But on the other hand, I would say that Richard Muller is a bit possessive, if he means by his statements that nobody that's not a hundred percent Reformed can rightly affirm the five points of Dort. I don't think that that's a logical argument, because Christians have been known—churches have been known—to pick and choose among theological traditions, exegetical traditions. And sometimes it may not seem logical to somebody else, but that's what they choose to affirm. I think that we have seen some evidence of too great a dependence on the Presbyterian system and this rash desire to have ruling elders in churches. The elder movement, I think, is a movement which has in a sense forgotten that this is one of the distinctives between Baptists and Presbyterians, and that we have not taken the position that ruling elders in the New Testament can be separated completely from teaching or preaching elders and so on. I would say that we have tended to cross the line in places and maybe have become too cozy with some parts of the Reformed tradition, which the early Baptists didn't. The early Baptists made some choices. They borrowed from this tradition heavily, but they also qualified it—and they qualified it on double predestination. Our documents at least have a doctrine of preterition instead of reprobation.

Mauldin: Right, sort of a passive passing over.

Garrett: We have not always taken the covenant of works and some of those other doctrines, and so Baptists, early Baptists, intentionally made some choices within that larger framework of the Reformed tradition. They were part of that tradition. I don't think you can understand Baptists, historically, if you take them completely out of that Reformed tradition. They don't belong in the Lutheran tradition. They don't belong in the Catholic of the Eastern Orthodox or even in the truest sense the Anglican tradition, because the Anglican tradition has some ecclesiology that Baptists have never adopted. So I would say that you have to start with recognizing that Baptists are part of that Reformed tradition, but they made deliberate choices from the earliest days, so that they would modify and even reject aspects of that Reformed tradition. That would be my answer, and that's what we should do today; we should respect the areas of common ground. And we've had our Calvinistic Baptists that have been in many ways the trunk line of Baptists historically, in both Britain and America. You can make an argument for that. There's hardly ever been a time when the Arminian Baptists outnumbered the Calvinists in America from the Great Awakening on, and yet, that Calvinism was very muted in the twentieth-century, very modified—almost lost, you might say. That's part of Tom Nettles's big argument, that it was lost, and Mullins and Scarborough were the two culprits, you know, they were the culprits. I didn't tell you—this is running a rabbit here—before we went to Canada, we went on a visit to Louisville. I taught at Southern Seminary fourteen years, and we still had friends there. I said to some people here, "We're going to visit our octogenarian friends in Louisville, Kentucky." Well, Tom Nettles heard of our coming and he asked me to lecture to his class on Baptist History. So I gave a lecture on Baptist identity and had an enjoyable time with his students. So, Tom and I would not agree on all points of theology, of course, but we had a very amicable and fraternal experience of lecturing to his class and hearing the questions of the students and answering them. So, I didn't get right on this point because I was dealing with other things, but I think even Nettles would recognize, has to recognize, that there were places where we broke with the Reformed tradition. I would see more breaks than he does—but the fact of breaks, yes.

Mauldin: The thesis that I'm writing for Southwestern is asking the question as to whether Andrew Fuller or Fullerism, is a better historical model than John Calvin or Calvinism, for the Baptists. Do you believe that there are issues—and I think we covered some of this in the first question, so this may be a brief answer—that there are some issues of soteriology, ecclesiology, and missiology—perhaps maybe missiology is an area that we didn't discuss before—that would make Fullerism a more appropriate Baptist designation or nomenclature? In other words, if I'm a Baptist, instead of saying I'm a Calvinist, perhaps maybe Fullerite would be a better historical landmark or some sort of nomenclature that makes more sense?

Garrett: I would say that you certainly have a point here, that Andrew Fuller was so much a part of the developing modern mission movement—gave so much energy and time to supporting the Carey mission and all of that—that this affected the way he preached and the way he did his writing and his theology. So I think that Fuller was impacted by missiology in a way that John Calvin was not. Now, it is true that Calvin had some connection with a small group of people that went to Brazil, and I'm sure you're familiar with that story. He seemed to give an encouragement to it—it was more a matter of, I think, some Europeans becoming colonists and settlers, maybe, than it was being missionaries. But, I think Calvin accepted the idea that the Great Commission had pretty well been fulfilled in earlier times, did he not? There is evidence of that. And so, it was the Anabaptists who were saying, "No"—sixteenth-century—"the Great Commission has not been fulfilled." So, I think that Calvin was not deeply motivated by what you would call any kind of missiological perspective or impulse. And Fuller was [motivated] more definitely, while holding to many of these points that have derived down from the Reformed tradition. Fuller did not write as much on ecclesiology as he did these other areas, and I don't think of Fuller as being so important for shaping Baptist ecclesiology as some other people. But, I think he had a Baptist ecclesiology, and that had to be related to his other doctrines. So yes, I think that you could make a point—make a case—for arguing that Fullerism, rightly understood, is a better model for Baptists today than strictly [Calvinism]—and here I am using Calvinism in the sense of the teachings of John Calvin. That's your question as I understand it. And you might be interested to know that when I gave a lecture for the B. H. Carroll Institute's colloquy a few days ago, in the question period, Dr. Corley, the President, raised the question, "What do you think of Andrew Fuller as a kind of important model for today?" That was his question he brought up, so I was able to tell him that I thought that he was an important milestone for Baptist theology, and as a pastor-theologian he had some important insights for us today. He was a prodigious worker, and yet he evoked great criticism from the followers of John Gill. And you had the Fullerites and the Gillites, and they battled one another, right? And the strict and Particular Baptists carried on that tradition of Gill, and so I am very much aware of that. And I think that Fuller has not been in the consciousness of most Baptists through the twentieth-century and into the twenty first-century. He's not one of the people that we've really taken seriously. And I think that's a mistake; I think he could have offered us more than we have taken from him. And I think basically—and here I don't want to sound too harsh—but I think that the Mullins tradition with soul competency and Christian experience has had such an impact on the twentieth-century—not just in recent years, but through all the twentieth-century—that we have not felt as Baptists the need of going back behind to earlier centuries to recapture our theological heroes. Now we're doing that. We started doing that with the George and Dockery book *Baptist Theologians* and the second edition, *Theologians in the Baptist Tradition*. And in those books we began to get our major theologians made available to the student and the pastor today in a way that hadn't been. And so, we're doing a better job now, and I think Fuller is understood perhaps today as being more important than would have been true, say, twenty five years ago. We weren't talking much about Fuller in the 1980s. I think that Fuller gave a theological rationale for those changes from hyper-Calvinism that enabled the missionary movement to exist and to thrive and to survive and to be supported. And I think that was very important. Now, he had some help to be sure, but I think that he was the major theologian of the new missionary thrust. We visited Kettering church a few years ago, still an active church there. And I thought about Fuller a great deal as we visited there.

Mauldin: In his historic work, *A Gospel Worthy of All Acceptation*, Fuller essentially argues that all men are duty bound to believe the Gospel. It seems that he was reacting to the hyper expressions of Calvinism that held to some sort of eternal justification and provided a rationale for not preaching the Gospel to sinners. In your opinion, was Fuller in disharmony with Calvin on this issue? Would Calvin have agreed with Fuller regarding man's duty?

Garrett: Chad, really to give you a good answer on this, I need to go back and read more sections of the *Institutes* to get my mind focused on the finer points of Calvin's treatments of some of those issues. It's been awhile since I've done that. But I certainly agree that he [Fuller] was reacting to hyper-Calvinism. You know, I sort of leave it as an open-ended question as to whether his home church at Soham was hyper-Calvinist or just high Calvinist, and I think there is a distinction there. A hyper-Calvinist would be John Gill, whom I regard as either three-fifths or four-fifths hyper-Calvinist. On the other hand, Abraham Booth would be or maybe Benjamin Keach would be a high Calvinist but not necessarily a hyper-Calvinist. So I don't know for sure about how to label the theology of his home church, but whether high or hyper, it was an atmosphere that inhibited a young man from readily making a profession of faith in Christ and seeking baptism. You were supposed to have a warrant, and that whole idea of the warrant was heavy on the hyper-Calvinists. It was a highly subjective sort of thing. You had to have an inner, experiential, assurance of being the elect before you could objectively overtly confess your faith in Christ. And I think that that greatly inhibited his becoming a believer, and he was slow to come to baptism because of that. Now, I think that whether Calvin ever addresses the question of duty to believe in the way Fuller did, I'm not sure that he ever addressed it in exactly the same way. I would have to read Calvin a lot more closely. Now, as far as things like eternal justification and no offers of grace, those were all hyper-Calvinist emphases. And by the way, I should point out here—I don't claim this in my book—but on page 89, I believe it is, I give these five tenets of hyper-Calvinism. I don't think anybody else has ever identified those as pointedly as I have. I didn't claim to be the first, because I wasn't sure. But you might want to take note of the possibility that my identification of those five as being parallel to the five of Dort—but different—those five marks of hyper-Calvinism provide some kind of measuring rod for determining whether a person was a hyper-Calvinist. If a man hit four out of five of those, you'd almost say that he hit the target. But if he only hit one of the five or two of the five, you might want to be hesitant to call him a hyper-Calvinist.

Mauldin: Is that the distinction you're making between hyper and high Calvinism—just someone that may hold to one to two of these points?

Garrett: No, not exactly. High Calvinism could be just a strong Dortian Calvinist, without necessarily taking these points. You know, there was some question about people like Knollys and Keach and those, whether they went too far as high Calvinists. They didn't seem to go as far as the hyper-Calvinists. They could preach for a person to believe and repent—to respond to the Gospel, seemingly.

Mauldin: That seemed to be the distinction, to call for a response.

Garrett: We talk about giving an invitation today. They would probably not use that kind of language. They would put it in different terms. And, they would not necessarily have an altar call. But, whether there is any section in Calvin that you could find that is even closely parallel to Fuller's argument, I don't know. I think that I would have to leave that open-ended, but I think that he [Fuller] was certainly reacting against hyper-Calvinism. That is certainly the case, and I don't think that Fuller really subscribed to any one of those five points of hyper-Calvinism. I think that the question revolves around how much of a Dortian Calvinist he was, not a question of hyper-Calvinism. But on Calvin, I'd have to go back. I just don't remember Calvin arguing for the duty of faith. Now he may somewhere, I just don't remember. I'm going to have to look for that.

Mauldin: Further research.

Garrett: Further research. I think that there's a possibility in some of his sermons or even some of his biblical exegesis that you could find a passage where he argues that point. But I'm not sure in the *Institutes* whether there is a section on that. And you know, the interesting point about Calvin, you can find some things in his sermons and his commentaries that are not discussed in the *Institutes*—one of which may be the question of limited atonement. I don't think he discussed that in the *Institutes*, but when he deals with some of the "all men" texts, he sounds like a general atonement man.

Mauldin: That's an old argument, right there.

Garrett: And some of the Calvinists really were upset with me for saying that in my Systematic Theology, but I think there's evidence for that. It wasn't a burning issue for Calvin's day. So he didn't have to come to a resolution of that issue. Later on, it became a burning issue, so I think we can't force Calvin into drawing conclusions that he didn't draw. That's my point.

Mauldin: Dr. Garrett, do you believe that a magisterial model for reformation or a sacral idea of society, somehow frustrates the notion of personal conversion? And if so, then could this have perhaps helped to prevent Calvin and others from developing what we call a modern doctrine of missions—this idea of magisterial reform or sacral society?

Garrett: Well, that certainly was the context in which John Calvin was working. But, as we mentioned earlier, the fact that he doesn't take the Great Commission as something yet to be fulfilled has to be looked at, along with the established church and infant baptism and all that he embraced. So yes, he was still working comfortably within the confines of the older Christendom. And that old Christendom involved the sacral society. And the *Corpus Christianum* society of Europe was a network of church and state and culture. There were dissidents to be sure, but the basic network was there, and, of course, the Reformation brought about a rupture in that. But basically there was still that idea of church and state and society that was very prevalent. And Calvin worked in that—accepted that—and you add to that then what I said about the Great Commission, and you don't have a missiological impulse, and you certainly don't have an idea of a gathered church on the basis of confession of faith. You have a doctrine of election, which is very powerful, but you have elect infants as well as elect adults. And so, yes, I think that for Calvin, personal conversion is not quite seen in the same sense. I think that the Great Awakening changed even our Baptist understanding of conversion. I think that although you could find one or two references in the English confessions of faith to being sure about admitting members into the church—I think that either the Midland or Somerset Confession says something about that—but I think the Great Awakening in New England and the Separate Baptists coming to the South made such a difference on the idea of conversion being so important. And also a called ministry, Backus was so emphatic about the church made up only of people who were truly converted, because he'd been an Old Light Congregationalist and then a New Light Congregationalist, then he'd become New Life Baptist. So he had made the whole trek, and, at the same time, he was very concerned about the fact that in New England there were pastors that didn't seem to be evidencing conversion and certainly not a call to ministry. So, he comes down heavily both on converted membership and a divine call to the pastoral office. Now, you had to have the church's call, to be sure, but you had to have a call from God. And I think that affected Baptist life very greatly in the beginning of that colonial period, coming on down in our Southern Baptist life. I remember my early days here, going across town and having an ordination exam for a seminary student. One of my colleagues here was in charge of the examination, and we went into that room and what do you think we did? We spent the whole hour on his conversion and his call, and the hour was up. We never got to any other questions. And I remember at the time I was sort of irritated by that. I thought, well why didn't we balance this thing a little bit better? But you know, as I look back on that—fifty years or more since that happened—we were doing a very Baptist thing that day. We were making absolutely sure about conversion and call, and if we didn't have that right, it didn't matter what he said about the other things. So my colleague was probably right, even though that day I was a bit irritated. Do you see what I'm saying?

Mauldin: I do.

Garrett: And so it's that personal conversion and call to ministry that has impacted Baptist life. And I don't know that Presbyterians—I'm not saying they can't have something like that, but for them it's not quite as acute. The Reformed tradition did not have it quite as acute in their psyches to emphasize these points. So you could have New England Congregationalism with the Half-Way Covenant and all that followed—you had a situation where a man got a nice job; he was a clergyman.

Mauldin: It was a career.

Garrett: Career, it was a career, and a very settled and safe career in New England to be a clergyman. So, that's an indirect way of answering some of your question here. I think that Calvin was a part of—very much a part of—the ecclesial and cultural and even political situation of his day and worked within that context and was not moved by Anabaptists or anybody else that wanted another position. This is not to say that Calvin is to be castigated. You know, I say in my book [*Baptist Theology*] that Spurgeon reveled in being a Calvinist. He thought that he was a true Calvinist, not after some of the modern deviations from Calvinism in his day.

Mauldin: Fuller thought the same thing.

Garrett: That's right they did, they both had some of that same idea. This is why I had to disagree a little bit with my friend Fisher Humphreys when he came out saying, you know, that the true Baptist line was not Calvinist. Well, where is the true Baptist line? If you don't have some Calvinism in that line, you've got a very crooked detour around some of the Baptist central lines. And you know, we have to be honest about our history. The first thing you have to do is be honest before you start working out today's problems. You certainly have to be fair with history, and that's what I think we must do. We must read these people as accurately as we can. Dagg was a Calvinist. I don't think Dagg bragged about being a Calvinist so much, but he obviously was. Boyce was a greatly devoted—

Mauldin: Charles Hodge's pupil in every sense of the word.

Garrett: Oh boy, pupil is right. There the work of Wiley Richards—you know this Wiley Richards who taught down at the school in Graceville, Florida, which is now, used to be called Baptist Bible Institute, is called Florida Baptist Theological College; I think something like that—he wrote on this area and really established pretty strongly and convincingly that Charles Hodge was the major shaper of much of James P. Boyce's theology, not his Baptist distinctives but most everything else. And that's true—and also the idea of a confessional seminary, having a confessional standard. Because Newton's seminary did not have a confession of faith, Brown University did not have a confession of faith, and Furman University didn't have a confession of faith. So when he proposed that the new seminary would have this *Abstract of Principles*, to which every professor was to adhere and sign and all that, he was following more the model of Princeton than he was Baptist institutions of his day. They did not actually require the same kind of signing. There's a heavy influence of Hodge, no question. So it's a matter of sorting it out, isn't it, Chad? There is a strong Calvinist strand, or Reformed strand there, but there have always been Baptist differences from the Reformed tradition—from the very beginning. And there have to be, if we're Baptist. I think you're to be commended for working on Fuller. He obviously was really an influential man in his day. He has been criticized. I think the worst book on Fuller is the one that I refer to in my treatment [*Baptist Theology*]. His name is Ella. Have you seen that book?

Mauldin: Yeah, I have it. Yeah, I don't know what to make of it. I mean, a lot of what he says, he doesn't note, and so I don't know what he's interacting with. You know, he'll just make some harsh statement about him [Fuller], but he won't tell me where he's interacting with Fuller, so I can't go there myself and interact with it and decide if I agree with him. He just says these things, at least a lot of these things.

Garrett: I have found him one of the most extreme writers that I had to deal with. I felt like he had an axe to grind, he knew before he started what he wanted to find. I am a bit suspicious of people who do research that way. They determine before they start what they're going to prove, and they bend all the evidence to prove it and they ignore some of the evidence that goes against it. I think it's a dangerous method myself, and I was a bit harsh with him, but I think he deserved it. In most cases, I let people speak and didn't try to correct them in my book, but with Ella I had to let it be known that it was extreme. I think Fuller deserves a better treatment than that.

Mauldin: Dr. Garret, you've been a tremendous help to me.

Garrett: Oh, I don't know that I've helped you much, Chad. But, we've had a good visit and I have enjoyed it.

Appendix B

A Selection of Andrew Fuller's Letters[1]

ANDREW FULLER TO WILLIAM CAREY: 9 AUGUST 1796

To Mr. Carey.
Kettering Augt. 9. 96.
My very dear Brother,

    I rec^d yrs. Dated Jany 12. 96 to me, accompanied with another of 3 sheets to the society, for all wh. I thank you. I am grieved that anything we have written sh^d have grieved you. You complain of my not writing. I think I must have written more than a Dozen Letters to you, and several of them very long ones. I am glad Bro^r. Morris is "copious". I will encourage him to be so still, and will do the best I can myself, tho' I have ten times the writing I suppose upon my hands that he has, and not half the capacity to perform it. Be assured my dear bro^r we are perfectly satisfied with your conduct. We have no suspicions of your being "indolent." Our cautions were not the result of any particular jealousy of you, any more than we sh^d have felt for any other person and perhaps not so much as in most other cases.

    You are "astonished that an Indigo Manufacturer sh^d be called a merchant". You seem to me to be answering Mr. Booth's Letter rather than that of the Society; for I do not find the word "merchant" in the latter. It is true there is mention made of your engaging "in the affairs of trade"; but this merely refers to the supposed share or partnership, and you yourself acknowledge that "were you <u>proprietors</u>, the name of

---

1. The following letters are a part of a larger body of Fuller's unpublished correspondence housed at Angus Library, Regents Park College, Oxford. This transcriber has reproduced the prepared manuscript without any intentional changes in spelling, punctuation, or content. Also, all superscripted letters throughout are a part of Fuller's shorthand. Furthermore, any footnotes henceforth marked with characters (not numerals) are to be understood as Fuller's notes, not editorials by this writer. These letters are used with the permission of the Angus Library and Archive, Regent's Park College, Oxford.

merchants might be proper.". We did not mean, my dr. bro^r to hurt your minds or grieve you, and we ourselves are grieved that the remittance in cutlery sh^d have been so long detained by the strange mistakes of dear Mr. Savage, of wh. I have this spring sent you a full account, and had you not been otherwise provided for we should have felt inexpressibly on acc^t of it. On these considerations we are not only satisfied, but thankful that you have engaged in business. We never thought of your being unemployed; and so far from thinking the worse of you for your willingness to do something to support yourselves, we are satisfied it arises fm. your disinterested regard to your undertaking. It was the <u>kind</u> of employment that excited a degree of fear, and this the Society stated in their letter, in wh. is a quotation from a letter from Mr. Thomas, sent fm. Hampstead to you Dec. 22. 92. stating the comparative influence of trade and husbandry upon the mind. And tho' we did not mean to censure you for anything, nor shall we think of doing so if you possess a share in the business; yet you must not wonder that we felt a degree of fear on your account.

You must also make some allowance for these fears on account of the strong language of the Londoners, by wh. for a time we were almost over-set. But you say "we ought to have boldly avowed that we expected you to engage in business of some sort." And I answer, <u>So we did</u>. I immediately answered the Walworth opinion upon your conduct in the strongest language I c^d devise in your favor, proving by references to your publication that this was always your plan, and that the Society agreed with you so to do. This letter had the desired effect. There has never been a word from that quarter, nor any other that I know of since that time, by the way of reflection. I believe that they were fully convinced by it that they had gone too far. And lest their sh^d be whispered about to your disadvantages I introduce the substance of my letter to Walworth into No. II of <u>Period</u>^{1}. <u>Acc</u>^{ts}, page 93 which has afforded universal satisfaction.

It is true there have been rumours from Tewkesbury to the disadvantage of the Mission, owing it is supposed, to Mr. Thomas's communications to his sister, in wh. it has been said, he invited his relations to go over, telling them that they might have £1000 a year when there. Except this, which seemed to imply that he himself was making a fortune, I have heard of no reflection upon either of you since the publication of No. II <u>Period</u>^{1}. <u>Acc</u>^{ts}.. And what, or whether any occasion was afforded for this by Mr. T. I don't know. I wrote to him however concerning it.

You may think we have treated the Londoners with too much tenderness, but the longer I live the more I see the necessity and the justice of setting no man down for an enemy till I have good evidence that he is one. As a proof that Booth & Thomas are cordial friends I will give you a short anecdote: About half a year ago poor Swain (who is since dead) with some other younger ministers in London made an attempt to have an Assistance Society in London, and proposed an annual meeting of the Society there. Booth & Thomas opposed it, and gave us their reasons wh. were to this effect: "if the Londoners form into a Society, they will have perhaps an ascendency in the management: you have hitherto conducted the business well, and why sh^d it come under other influence?" We could not but admire this disinterested advice. For my part as soon as the proposal was made I saw what wd. be the consequence if it succeeded; and therefore told Booth in a letter to this effect: "Though we had no jealousy from the love of power, yet justice to our brethren who were gone out upon our assurances of never deserting them, required that we should not give up the management, nor ascendancy in it." With this Booth & Thomas concurred, & therefore opposed the plan. Booth also undertook to conciliate Swain and others wh. was happily effected. Even Dore & Keen & Giles, notwithstanding they erred that once, have ever since been very friendly, and give us all the help they can. Keene I think is not long lived; & Dore has had something of the apoplectic kind, so as greatly to affect him.

Some months ago Bro^r Sutcliff agreed to send you a quantity of seeds &c and accordingly spoke to Maddock of Walworth to execute the order, promising him ready money for them; and wh. we agreed to advance on your account. That order will be completed and go I expect this season. So Mr Maddock assured me it sh^d when I was at Walworth about 6 weeks ago. And now as the water has destroyed you indigo plant; and you cannot assure us that Boulton would meet with any employ of a secular kind, if he were to come, we conclude it may be the same by Tronlaks. We therefore shall allow the value of the seeds for his support the first year, together with 4 guineas wh. Bro^r Sutcliff has paid for Parkhurst's lieb. & Gr. Lexioons wh. he has sent you. Or if he sh^d not need it, apply it in some way to the promotion of the mission, or reserve it for the expense of printing. We expected according to your last Letters to receive Letters for types. Whenever we receive them I expect we shall cordially unite with you in that work. I do not fear for the want of money. Only take great heed that it be as accurate as possible. It is not for want of money that we cannot send out more missionaries, but of <u>suitable characters</u>. That is a matter of great importance. A Wesleyan mission to the Tronlaks in Africa has failed this last year owing to this. When they came to meet difficulties they refused to go any farther. We had better wait than send unsuitable persons. Bro^r Ryland thinks that the Lama of Thibet, and heathen popery will be as great a bar to a mission there as can exist in Spain or Portugal but we may have wrong ideas at this distance.

ANDREW FULLER TO WILLIAM CAREY: 6 SEPTEMBER 1797

To Mr. William Carey, Mudnabatty, near Malda, Bengal.
Kett^g. Sept. 6. 1797
My very dear brother,

I duly rec^d y^{rs} to me of Nov. 16. 96, and at the same time ano^r to the Society f^m Hooghly River Dated Dec. 28. 96. They arrived July 25. 97. It affords us great pleasure to hear of the hopeful appearances at Moypaul and Mudnabatty. The L^d. grant they may abide! - - - At the same time we feel for your situation in temporaly.

At a committee Meet^g held here on Aug. 29. 97, at wh. were present Bre^n Sutcliff, Pearce, Blundel, Morris, Pane, Evans, Hogg, and several of our own frds, the follow^g Resolutions passed—(These resolutions relate to effectual pecuniary and

I. That our bre^n hav^g in a disinterested manner declined their ordinary income f^m us, at a time when they thought they cd. do without it; and various unforeseen circumstances having since occurred, wh. render it necessary that we shd. afford them substantial assistances, Resolved, that at this time we will pay them those arrears, wh. for a time they have voluntarily declined—that is, that we will make up what has been sent out in goods at different times, £100 to each family, for 4 years, viz fm. Nov. 7. 93 to Nov. 7. 97.

II. That 50£ be added to the above for Bro^r Fountain f^m the time of his arrival to Nov. 7. 97.

N.B. That account of Monies Paid, and goods already sent out is as follows- - - - -
To goods taken with you 150.0.0
To shoes, hose, &c. sent May 94   40.0.0
To Druggs . . . . ditto   10.0.0
To Cutlery sent May 96 . . . . .   145.6.0

To Cash pd. Mr. Savage as Mr. Thomas's agent to make the last 3 Articles
£210.0.0.   14.14.0
To seeds sent Oct. 96   50.0.0
To Cutlery now ready for sail^g 175.0.0
To Druggs to be added to the last Article 'ere it sails   25.0.0.
Besides the above I have given orders for light Woolen Cloaths 50£ Shoes 50£ Stationary 50£ Hatts & Hose 40£
The other 50£ I shall reserve till I hear from you by the last ships, Or shall send it in seeds by the Spring ships.
Alltogether will make - - - - - - - - -
240.0.0.

850.0.0.

These goods, the whole of wh. have gone or will go within about 6 weeks, (except the 50£ reserved for Seeds and w^h will go early in the Spring)—answer to your four years Income of 100 pnds. each & 50£ for Bro^r Fountain. It is probable however that in executing the last Orders they may amount some to a little more & some less, than the exact sums, wh. will be seen by the invoices.

 III. That we feel anxiously concerned to comply with Bro^r Carey's request of send^g more missionaries, but that at present there is either a want of suitable persons, or such difficulties in the way of those who are, such as cannot be surmounted."—

 N.B. <u>Mr. & Mrs. Yates</u> have been a good deal exercised about it: but they do not appear to be willing—otherwise we wd. gladly send them. He has broke a blood vessel, and is afraid of the sea sickness & other things. We cd. not urge it upon them. Yet, Mrs. Y. seemed in a most desirable state of mind concerning it. <u>Bro^r Read</u> would be a suitable person and was present at our meet^g. But his wife and eldest daughter are not willing. And his family is so large that it is a very serious matter on <u>their</u> acc^t, as well as on acc^t of the expence. I suppose Voyage and preparations cd. not cost so little as 700£. We did not absolutely determine agns^t sending them on account of the expence, tho' considering the work of printing the N.T. as before us, we hesitated. But the unwillingness of his wife, and the consideration that she had formally been in a very unhappy state of mind, and that you seemed to want active woman, were at present an absolute bar.—Mr. Boulton in Gloucestershire, bro' Ryland says, is so flat and uninteresting a character, that he w^d not do. We might probably have Mr. Rodway, who returned last October f^m Africa on acct. of ill health; but the hot climate kills him. And he is so flat in his spirits that you wd. never hear him speak from morning to night, except in answering a question.

As to your plan of uniting families we have nothing to object. The experience of the Moravians seems to sanction it. But I suppose you cd. not carry it into execution without more missionaries, and without some active amiable woman amongst them. Do whatever you judgment dictates, all circumstances considered. So advises the Society. We will give you every assistance in our power. As to the place, whether about Nuddea, or Northwood, for the reasons you have given incline to the latter. You speak sometimes of being obliged to quit the C^{os} territories. Sh^d you be safer on the territories of any of the Eastern princes? You must judge of this, and indeed in all these things you must ultimately judge for yourself. We have great confidence in your prudence.

You wish us to "ascertain the sum you shall receive; & to fix on a plan of sending it; also a plan for receiving your donations to the Mission."

As to the first. If you continued in separate families, we do not wish to allow you less than we have done 100£ to each family, and 50£ to Bro^r Fountain while he continues single & with you—And more in case it be wanted. But if you execute your plan, we do not think it best to fix your allowance till you can tell us the expenses fm actual experiment. We hope that the goods voted to be sent out will supply your wants—Having paid Mr. Thomas his share use the rest as you judge proper. Whatever plan you pursue we hope this will at present suffice.

Secondly, As to the plan of sending you supplies, we shall certainly adopt that of sending goods as being the most advantageous to you. Whatever advantage arises from the sale of the Articles belongs to the Missionaries.

Lastly, for the sake of ease and order in paying and rec^g monies, it is the desire of the Society that you should be considered as their Treasurer in India. All our remittances will be to you. Keep a regular account of D^r & C^r with us, and send it us in every February or March, wh will arrive in July or August in time to make up our Annual Accts. Whatever Donations you give set yourself down Dr. and receive the Donation of others. To this Acct. set down what you have advanced for Bro^r Fountain's extra Voyage expences. We hope for the present Broʳ F. may assist in the education of your children &c.

You say Garden seens² shd. arrive in Sep. or Oct. We will endeavor that they shall do so if possible: but Broʳ Sutcliff says your orders were different last time—and that consequently the last parcel of Seeds were sent in Oct, & wd. arrive in the Spring.

In the orders wh. are now executing every parcel of goods will be attended with an Invoice and a Copy sent to you in a Letter—All will be sent <u>to the care of Tulloh & Co. Calcutta.</u>

Besides these there will be a parcel of <u>books</u>—Schmidts Greek Concordance—Montanus's Heb. Bib. Some arabic books wh. were bought for the African Mission, but now are to be sent to you, with a number of other pieces. I am sorry for the loss of the Polyglot Bible &c. but we must not give them up yet. You say "a friend made enquiry for the Polyglot bible at the Custom House," but did he enquire for <u>a chest directed to Mr. Thomas or yourself</u>? The chest might be there at the same time, and the people at the Custom House might know nothing of its contents. You had no fixed residence at the time that was sent therefore I suppose it was not directed so as to find you. You speak of Mr. Thomas's "Chest of Medicines" along with it as being lost. But by the Accᵗ of goods sent out in page 1. you will see we never sent out any Medicines but once, viz. in May 94 and of them you acknowledged the arrival.

As to printing the N.T. with Genesis and a few other portions of the Old Tesᵗ. We can do nothing until we receive Letters for patterns of Types. But how is it that these cannot be found in printed books and wh. wd. be more certain than written ones? Does not Halhed's Grammar contain all the Letters & characters in the Bengal language?

You propose 10,000 copies, and all to be <u>given away</u>. To us it seems the wisest thing to sell them, as cheap as may be. People seldom feel interested in that wh. costs them nothing. Those who cd. afford it wd. purchase them; and to those who cd. not many might be given awa. But as in other matters, you must best know the circumstances of people around you.

You wonder at their being no formal recommendation of Broʳ Fountain fᵐ the Society. Mr. F. at first proposed going on his own accᵗ, and as a captain's servant. It was at this time that the Society met; and we

---

2. Transcriber's note: It appears contextually that this word should be read as "seeds."

did not consider him then as a regular missionary, only proposed to see him in his passage, as we tho't him likely to be useful to the Mission. But when he was disappointed of a passage in the way that was expected, I wrote to the acting members of the committee for their judgment relative to his going out as a regular missionary, and at the Society's expence—To wh. they all cheerfully agreed. Soon after this I went to London, and a ship being obtained for his passage, there was no time for me to call another Committee Meet^g. I therefore thought it sufficient to write to you in the name of the Society recommending him as a person whom we approve. And this I did in a letter wh. I either sent by him or by another ship a little before him, I am not certain which.

You desire us to keep your spelling in what we print. We will endeavor to do so but you do not always spell alike. Sometimes you write Moonshee, & sometimes Munshi, and sometimes Moonshi. If the trumpet give uncertain sound, who can prepare for battle?—You must allow me again to remind you of your punctuation. I never knew a person of so much knowledge as you profess of other languages, write English so bad. You huddle half a dozen periods into one. Where your sentence ends you very commonly make only a semicolon instead of a period. If your Bengal N.T. sh^d be thus pointed I sh^d tremble for its fate.

The last accounts of Bro^r Thomas were encouraging. We sh^d have been glad to have heard f^m him by these ships.

I saw your father a few weeks since. He was very well. Your sister Polly is very ill. They don't expect her to live long. Things go on very well with most of our churches. Arnsby & Clipstone Meet^g Houses must come down for the sake of enlargement, and perhaps ours may soon follow their example. I baptized 6 lately, & expect 10 or 11 more shortly. North-ton is yet unprovided; yet they prosper. Mr. Booth has written a book wh. he will send you, and Mr. Scott ano^r agnst it wh. also will be sent. Mr. B's book is controversial, but very difficult to know who or what it opposes. What he aims to establish in the former part is denied by nobody that I know of except the High Calvinists—Yet he did not mean I am persuaded to oppose them. So however that part of his work is generally understood. People reckon, and so let them reckon, that his book is on the same side as my <u>Gospel of Xt</u> &c. I believe it was his intent to oppose our Sentiments, and that he chose to attack us under Hopkins's name. The latter part I think is erroneous.^{X} The whole is subject to many

    X. He asserts, no holy disposition is necessary in order to come to Xt. "I ansr No man can come but whom the Father <u>draws</u> and he draws <u>the will to Xt</u>. No person therefore while in he is unwilling, or wh. is same thing, void of all holy disposition, can come to Xt."

animated versions. But you will read it & judge for yourself. Mr. Scotts piece I have not yet read. There are some young gifts rather promising in Talgrave Ch. & who supply at Moulton, Sheepshead & Leic^r ch's have had troubles only to a Mr. Carrat, but things I hope are coming round. Cave is a ing[3] man. Grigg who has given us such great trouble is in spite of all we cd. say or do, gone from Sierra Leone to America. So our African Mission is at an end. Tim^y Thomas resides now at Islington—has lately lost his wife and his venerable father dr-T. of Leominster—You request a balance to be paid to Mr. Sutcliff for books & debt wh. you owed him when you left England. We do not think of charging the books to you; and as to the debt that has been settled years ago. Our friends Wallis, Timms, Gotch, Hobson &c &c. to whom you sent kind remembrance beg theirs in return to you & yrs. The brethren at the Committee meet^g desire the same. My two oldest children, Robert about 15 and Mary about 11 desire their love to Felix & such other of your children as can read, and request their acceptance of some little books wh. they will put into the parcel of books. You will also present my love to your worthy friend and patron, and intreat his acceptance of my <u>L^{rs} on Socin^m -</u> with the <u>Defense</u> of them bound up together, as a small token of gratitude for his great kindness towards you and the Mission. Present all our most affect^{te} remembrance to Breth^n Thomas, Powell, Long, & all their families—to Mohun Chund, Parbottee, if with you, to Sookman and Yardee & Cassinut, and all who love our Ld Jes. Christ in sincerity. We long to hear of their hav^g <u>put on Xt.</u>

You may be sure we shall attend to y^r request about missionaries if possible, but the no. of suitable persons willing to go is so few, as one cd. not have supposed without trial—I hope when you went to Calcutta on Dec. 96 you found at Tullop & Cos the Cask of Cutlery that sh^d have come in 94 but wh. went in the <u>Royal Admiral</u>, Capt. Fellows in May 96, and that ere this reaches you you will also have rec^d the <u>Seeds</u> which went out in Oct 96. Mrs. Fuller unites in love to Self & M^{rs} C with your affect. Bro^r.

A. FULLER

---

3. Transcriber's note: There appears to be some missing text here.

ANDREW FULLER TO WILLIAM CAREY: 18 APRIL 1799

To Mr. Carey, Mudnabatty, near Malda, Bengal.
Kett^g 18 Ap. 99.
My very dear brother Carey,

I yesterday sent off a letter to you apprising you of the missionaries sailing about the 14th of May, and proposing that you sh^d meet them at Serampour. I now begin another sheet which I may fill up before they depart as subjects occur.

No Letters yet rec^d f^m you this Spring. I was lately at Mr Powells, St. Jno Street 178. If you give him an order annually for a few Articles, as you proposed to me, he will send them with the parcel for his son. His parcel is gone this Spring. The missionaries will bring with them a few pieces of cloth for coats, & velveteen for small cloaths. I gave your order for seeds &c. to Maddock & Son, Walworth, last autumn requesting them to have a parcel ready this spring: but they have given over business. Wright, their successor, says he cannot execute it this spring; but by autumn he will do it. The fruits of Mr Ryland's labours at Bristol appear to good purpose, not only in a number of spiritual young men in the Academy, but in so charming a group of missionaries, as are now going. Bro Sutcliff has baptised 9 lately. He is appointed to supply you with books; and I doubt not but he will magnify his office. Pearce is a wonderful Christian. He preached here last autumn like an Apostle from Ps. 90.16,17. Hall who preached after him was dismayed at the thoughts of following him, not so much at an idea of inequality of talents but of spirit and unction. But whether we shall ever hear him again God only knows. Booth is very asthmatic, & can preach but little. <u>We</u> have had but little increase of late, but hope there are some stirrings. Some of our most amiable and intelligent young men are obliged to the town for want of trade. Two of them (the Burditts) are gone to London, and have joined Mr. Booth. I am much better as to my complaint in the head, but never expect to be well. The labours attended in sending out of these missionaries overdo me. My head at this time is very poorly. Letter writing, and the anxious cares of the whole undertaking lies heavy upon me; & the heavier on acc^t of bro^r Pearce's affliction. It is well for him that bro^r Morris has set up printing; as it eases him of arranging and printing the Per. Acc^{ts}.; but that now in part falls on me. Morris will shortly begin to print my work ag^t Infidelity, and wh. I entitle: <u>The Gospel its own witness: or the holy nature & divine harmony of the Christian Religion.</u> I sometimes say Woe is me, for I am born to be a man of strife! Here are Arminians, Socinians, & final Restitutionists always provoking me to write. I seem like a sort of pugilist, who having made a little noise in the world draws upon himself every one that fancies he can master him. In truth I am obliged to overlook many things in periodical publications; and content myself without having the last word in controversies. Sometimes my heart sicks with contention: and yet I cannot forbear contending, and earnestly too for I hope the faith once delivered to the saints. Dr. Jenkins has lately attacked me in the Protestant Dissenters Mag. on Justification; and I have given him a full answer; and in so doing have answered some things in Booths <u>Glad Tidings</u> &c. I have also reviewed Scotts <u>Warrant and Nature of Faith</u> in the Evan. Mag. & wh. I expect will be inserted next number in wh. the controversy between them is summed up, and stated as clearly as I was able. These pieces you have had sent you, & the review you will see. Village preaching is diligently followed up, & and I hope with some success. I never thought that Godwin on political justice a work of merit, and that the virtue he pleads for sh^d be named on the same day with that of Edwards. He is a lewd character; and his work is condemned even by the French reviews as disorganising and inconsistent with human happiness.

I have never been deeply versed in the prophecies. There are some things however wh. have appeared to me with clearness, and which respect the present times. It appears that Anti-Xt or the <u>man of sin</u> may be said to have a body and spirit. By its body I mean civil power, and wealth &c called the flesh of the whore; by its spirit its doctrines, superstitions &c. The first of these was given it by the powers of the earth, and is to be taken away by those who gave it. Rev. 17. 13, 16. or rather is already taken away in a great degree, and probably will go on in the same course till it is completed. It is no objection to this that they are <u>kings</u> who gave and republicans who have taken away: for the term king in prophetic language does not mean governor of a particular form, but a <u>power</u> whatever be the form of it. Republican Rome is called a king in prophesy Dan. 7. 17. It were the powers of Europe that gave their kingdoms to the beast, of wh. France took the lead; and it will be by the same powers taken away, & here also France has taken the lead. Of the papal or little horn it is said <u>they</u> shall take away his dominion, to consume and to destroy it unto the end. Dan vii.26, which words denote that it shall be done by <u>force of arms</u>—and that it sh^d be gradually accomplished.—As to the soul or spirit of anti-Xt, it began to work in the apostles' days; and as it was produced and promoted by Falsehood, it will fall by the truth. Christ will destroy it by the spirit of his mouth and the brightness of his coming. Here then is our province. We must aim our weapons at its heart and soul, while the powers of the earth from carnal motives are burnish its flesh.

Ap. 20. Since writing the above I have been to Olney, to advise with bro^r S. about missionary concerns; and lo, while I was there in bolted Carey! Do not be alarmed: it was not your angel, but what did our hearts more good than if it had. It was your letter of Oct. 10. 98. On return I found a packet from bro^r F. and yourself, dated from May 30 to Oct. 30. 98. Well, God always causeth us to triumph. He is making room for you in India. Blessed be God for giving you favour in the eyes of men; and still more for giving you hopes of some of them being real Xns! I will write if I can a miscellaneous things in reply to yours and bro^r F's Letters before our brethren go off; and as these letters will go by them I shall feel at liberty to drop a few things in ans^r. to bro^r F. on politics, having no fear of their being opened before they arrive. I shall sometimes talk to bro^r F. and sometimes to you; and thus he must consider me as writing to him. We have bought a press and English types with a little Heb. & Gr. But if not wanted you can dispose of them.

Well, bro^r F. you have said that you do not trouble yourself about[4] yet in the same letter talked of K.G. being a Solomon . . . or rather on your judgment a Rehoboam! Are you not like some men who have been so long in the habit of swearing, that they do not know when they do swear? Or rather like one that sh^d swear that he does not live in that practice. Seriously, it is <u>wise</u> that you sh^d hazard perhaps the existence of the Mission for the sake of sneering at the K. or "HONOURABLE COMPANY"? See and seriously consider Eccle^s. X. 20. But it is not unwise only, but in my judgment <u>unrighteousness</u>. You are required by the N.T. to <u>pray</u> for all that are in authority: but this you cannot do without mockery unless you bear good will towards them, and that in their <u>official</u> capacity. It is written, thou shall not speak evil of the ruler, (or rulers) of the people; but to deal in sarcastic reflections upon them is the worst kind of evil speaking and is utterly inconsistent with the practice of Xt and his apostles. Do you not think that Paul & Peter & Jude could have found fools & tyrants among the rulers of their day? Yet, they never

---

4. Transcriber's note: A word or phrase is omitted from the manuscript here.

say anything disrespectful of the powers that were, nor allowed it in Xns. On the contrary, they described the <u>liberty boys</u> of that day in a light wh. sh^d make us tremble how we join with our approve of them in ours. 2 Pet. II. 10. Jude 8, 9, 10. You "are not ignorant of many in India being dissatisfied with the Company"—very likely: and I am not ignorant of many in England who are the same with the gov^t, & who I believe w^d not only be glad to see things reformed but utterly overturned, but I never give encouragement to such talk, much less join it. I am not an old man; but I have lived long enough to perceive that 9 out of 10 who are clamorous for liberty only wish for <u>a share in the power</u>; and follow them into private life and you will find them tyrants to their wives, children, servants and neighbors. I have observed also that those ministers who have been the most violent partizans for democratic liberty; are commonly not only cold hearted in religion, but the most imperious in their own churches. Now whatever faults I may see in the gov^t of my country, I had rather be under it as it is than under such kind of liberty as I sh^d have reason to expect from such characters. I have seen enough of French liberty to be fully convinced that, however there were well meaning individuals among them, whose object was justice, & the melioration of the state of mankind, yet the great body of the leading men, and by whose influence all the rest were led, were unprincipled infidels, whose object was to climb over the throne and get the supreme power, and to root up not merely popery but the very existence of Xnty. And now they have got the supreme power in France their object is to extend it over Europe, and even the whole earth. And I am much inclined to think that the 11th Chapter of the Rev. wh. speaks of the witnesses to be slain a little before their resurrection, & the kingdoms of the world becoming the kingdom of the Lord and of his Xt is near at hand—and that the peoples & kindred that shall rejoice over them will be the Infidel party, who shall exult that they have overturned Xnty, & crushed the sect of the Nazarenes. I am aware that this rejoicing is ascribed to "the beast"; from whence Dr. Gill concluded that "popery should once more be the prevailing religion of Christendom." But I believe he was mistaken. The present infidel government is only a part of branch of the papal. It has grown out of it and therefore is reckoned as belonging it. I am strongly inclined to believe that it will be very short in its duration. It has not an individual subsistence given it in the system of prophecy. The gov^{ts} of Bab. Persia, Macedon, & Rome, were Beasts, and all their subdivisions are pointed out: but the great empire of France is not mentioned. It is not a beast but a kind of cancerous excrescence growing out of the body of the papal beast, which will prove the death of that on which it grew, but itself will die with it. There is no duration allowed by prophesy between the fall of Babylon and the Kingdom of Xt. It will I think be hardly a nine days wonder. If after it has destroyed the papal power in Europe, and perhaps with it the Mahomedan, it survive 3 days & a half to "make merry" I expect it will be all. Whether when the power shall be given to the people of the S^{ts} of the most High, (by wh. I understand all places of power & trust being filled with true Christians) the government of the nations will be monarchical or Democratical I neither know nor care: nor do I believe that the scriptures consider it as of any account. Whether one man be called a king, and advises with others around him—or 500 men be called a Council, a Congress, or a Parliament, and who, by the bye, are certain to be influenced by two or three leading characters . . . . to me appears a small affair, and beneath the attention of God's word: but whatever be the form, Justice, goodness, peace & happiness will distinguish its administration. Here then is our work, to spread the gospel. Peace on earth will never be found till this is accomplished. War may be ascribed by designing demagogues to kings, and all hue and cry be raised ag^t them among the populace, but war arises from the lusts of ambition, revenge &c. which are in all men by nature, and which when they are exalted to places of power will make their appearance, whether they be kings or directors, or prime ministers. Those who ascribe all war to kings and thereby excite the people to hate them are at the very time wishing and promoting a civil war in the heart of their country, in order that they may get more power by the change. This is a time, & may be <u>the hour</u> of temptation wh. is coming upon all the world to try them that dwell upon the earth. I think also with Lowman and Edwards that this is the time of the pouring out of the VI vial. Rev. 16. 12–16. and which is accompanied with this emphatic warning to the servants of God, "Behold I come as a thief. Blessed is he that <u>watcheth and keepeth his garments</u>, lest he walk naked and they see his shame!"

Towards the beginning of this letter I was saying something about prophesy. I will add I think Bell of Wooler in the Evan. Mag. Vol. IV p53, 98. has written excellently upon the passage just quoted, but I think he is mistaken in part on that as well as in some other particulars. I will copy a few of my notes which I made on him at the time.

p. 57. on Dan. VIII. 13, 14. Query, Does this apply to Anti-Xt? It seems rather spoken of the mischiefe of Antiochus Epiphanes, wh. tho' typical of, or as I sh^d rather say, analogous to those of paper Anti-Xt; yet everything wh. is said of the one is not designed to be applied to the other. All that he writes in p. 58 seems to me to refer only to Antiochus. This little horn was said to have place under the third or Macedonian Monarchy, signified by a He-goat; whereas the papal AntiXt was under the 4th or Roman.

p. 60, line 18. "Remained in the Jewish church will the death of Xt." Was it not taken away then by Antiochus?

p. 101 on Rev. 16. 12. I see no fitness in making superstition the Euphrates of the N.T. Babylon. It seems to be not so much a guard and supply of Babylon as a component part of her. Query. Is not <u>the union of Church and State</u> that to the N.T. Bab. Wh. Euphrates was to the old? Is it not by her union with the Civil power that she is guarded & supplied? And when this union is dissolved there the Euphrates is dried up, and the city taken. Many Expositors have looked for some "Eastern King" to invade the papal power: but the whole is an allusion to the taking of old Bab. it is sufficient that they were kings of the east who took the old city. The city now to be taken is not a literal one but a community extending over many nations: The river to be dried up is not a literal river, but something analogous to what Euphrates was to Bab: and the kings of the east are not literal kings but people who shall do to N.T. Bab. as the kings of the east did to the old.

Bro^r Carey's conjectures of the Hindoos being descended from the 10 tribes appears to me utterly inadmissable. The Hindoos were the same people in the time of Alexanders invasion as now, tho' this was soon after the 10 tribes were led captive.

There has been a proposal for a Vol. of Sermons to be printed as a monument of friendship under some such title as this: <u>Sermons on Important Subjects by several Ministers of the Baptist denomination.</u> One or two may be furnished by Sutcliff—Ryland—Pearce (if he sh^d live!)—Fuller—Steadman &c. It will not be done very soon. Could Bro^r Carey write out and send <u>one sermon</u> at least—one of the most interesting that he has preached to the Hindoos, that his respected & beloved name may be united with that of his brethren?

Now my dear bro^r F. let this be the last letter in wh. I shall have occasion to write to you on a certain subject. Our brethren who are coming to join you, Bro^r Ryland says, are not infected with "the political mania". Deal not in sarcastic sneers ag^t the government be it what it may by wh. you are protected. Give no offense to Jew or Gentile, governed or governors. If you still think however that this sarcastic way of thinking, speaking & writing is consistent with the duty of a Christian, and a missionary, avow it fairly & you and I will discuss the subject as Brethren on Scripture grounds. We all love you. Only cultivate good will towards men, and a respect towards civil government whether it be in the hands of kings, company directors, or who it may, and all will be well. Read Titus 3, 1,2,3. Write to me as often as you can. I am a dull flint, you must strike me ag^t a steel to produce fire. Ask me as many questions as you please. I do not engage to answer all; but those that I like I will do what I can to answer. Be assured I have done all I c^d f^m the time you left England to encourage Miss T. to come to you; and now I expect she is going, the Lord go with her and bless you both! Many in England and Scotland think & speak very respectfully of you, who if they had seen all your letters w^d for ought I know have withdrawn their support from a missionary society who continued to employ such a missionary. David Dale of Glasgow, a most excellent man, who gives us unsolicited 20 guineas per annum & 50£ extra for the Translation, wrote to me on hearing of some of Griggs squabbles "Have your missionaries to learn that Xts Kingdom is not of this world?"

So I see by a letter f^m bro^r Ryland you are puzzled about the serpent eating <u>dust</u>. It does not mean that it should <u>be</u> his food, and that he sh^d eat it of choice; but that he sh^d <u>adhere</u> to his food, and he sh^d eat it against his choice; and this is a necessary consequence of going upon <u>his belly</u>. Men when fallen are said to <u>lick the dust like a serpent</u>. Ps. 72.9., Mic. 7.17. The French have of late adopted a phrase when speaking of the slain in battle; they say they have "bit the dust". Each of these applications of the word denotes involuntary abasement; and none of them that dust is eaten or licked or bitten by choice.

Bro^r F. is puzzled with the book of Job. There is a fine, poetic paraphrase of that book by a Mr. Scott with critical notes. Bro^r Sutcliff has sent it to you. The author I think was a stranger to the gospel, yet you will (think) it a work of great value; perhaps equal to Lowth on Isaiah.

Ap. 25. 99. Since writing the above I have rec^d from bro^r Read Mr. F's letters to him and Mr. Pullin. I find both Read and Pullin are much alarmed at their contents considering them as highly dangerous, and the more so as Read says "All the letters have been opened before they came." Pullin is greatly hurt, and expects disagreeable consequences to himself & his acquaintance. To me the whole appears as sinful as it is unwise. If Mr. F. be so infatuated with political folly, as not to be able to write a letter to England without sneering sarcasms upon Gov^{ts}, "cursing" their monopolies, expressing his hopes of revolution work going on &c &c I must say once for all, It is my judgment that the Society, much as they esteem him in other respects, <u>will be under the necessity of publickly disowning him</u>, as they were obliged to disown Grigg. There seems indeed to be much truth in what he says to Mr Read that he sh^d consider an alteration of his notes as a greater crime than "<u>treason</u>"! But how this can be reconciled with Christianity I know not. Pullin is disgusted at those parts of the letter to him wh. breathe a democratic phrenzy: and I think it is proof of his being a man of good sense. A little knowledge makes a man half mad: a good deal sobers him. Pullin has not been without thoughts of writing a letter to Mr F. fully <u>disowning</u> the revolutionizing motives and tendencies of their Musical Society wh. he ascribes to it and of sending it by post, <u>in hope</u> of its being opened as well as F's, and wh. would clear him: but has been dissuaded from it by Read. I cannot help observing the carnal tendency of Bro^r F's politics upon his own mind. All his letters to his old political acquaintances are as void of religion as they well can be. He tells Pullin "he wishes him to be a partaker of the Gospel", it is true, but the spirit breathed in the Letter from first to last has no tendency to make him think well of the gospel, but to harden him in a contrary spirit to it. Some parts of it were frothy, and others (I mean that which relates to politics) detestable.

 I need not say after this that I feel indignation in reading his Letter to Pullin.... I feel for the cause of God. My heart weeps for its wounds! Yet I could weep also over Bror. F. I am sure I love him dearly. His hymn on 2 Cor. VI.1. delights and affects me. I believe I once told him he was a rhymist not a poet: but I am now half inclined to alter my opinion of him. I see in him a young man of promising abilities, lively ingenious, open, disinterested, diligent, in a word amiable: but infatuated by a little superficial knowledge of governments, infused into him by such designing demagogues as Thelwall, whose infidel hearts sought not the good of mankind, but their own aggrandisement.

 In England serious people have mostly recovered from the infatuation with wh. many of them were affected; and are receding from those subjects to their proper standard, the Kingdom of Xt. Those who persevere in them are generally gone or going fast off to the standard of infidelity. A genuine zeal for Xt and a revolutionizing spirit cannot subsist long together. Xty breathes peace, modesty, good will to men, respect for civil government; and if it disapprove of particular men and measures, it will be with concern and not with "curses", sarcastic sneers, or noisy declamation. Here I could gladly end with a wish to say no more on this unpleasant subject. Let Bro^r F. try his spirit by the word of God; and he will repent and abhor himself in dust and ashes. Could I see this I sh^d be ready, if possible, to fly to India & embrace him in my arms. The Lord Jes.Xt. be with his spirit. It is possible that as his letters appear to have been opened we may shortly hear of it, and be reduced to the necessity of either disowning any further connection with him, or seeing the whole undertaking ruined! If, as you said, it was "very wrong in Grigg to sacrifice the cause of God at Sierra Leone to a political wrangle"; much more this in India to an itching for Discharging a few political squibs, without any good end whatever to be answered by them! It is a painful circumstance that this sh^d be the period when Miss T. sh^d be going out, and it is possible that soon after she is gone we may be under the painful necessity of disowning and recalling him! Brother Fountain! You have been playing so long at the mouth of the cockatrice's den that he seems to you harmless. Spare thyself! Or if you have no regard to yourself, spare that cause wh. is worth thousands of such lives as yours and ours! Repent, Repent, & ere it be too late, if it is not now too late!

Alas, alas! Our dear bro^r Pearce! He gets worse every week. Soon I fear we shall see his face no more. I am distressed for thee, my bro^r Pearce! Very pleasant hast thou been to me & to many more. O my bro^r Pearce! Thou hast fallen a sacrifice to thy unremitted labours! But O blessed man, what a frame of mind does he possess!

May 6. Miss T. and her father and mother are now at Kett^g come to take leave of her. She does not weep at parting from her friends, but she does on acc^t of M^r F's letter to Mr Pullin & she is far from happy. She fears I know, not from what I have said to her, but from a previous conversation with Bro^r Read that Mr F. with all his qualifications which she certainly does not undervalue, will bring himself to her ruin! May the Lord prevent her fears and ours also! We are now going to Olney—to London & can therefore add no more but that I am my dear brethren ever <u>yours</u> in the bonds of tenderest regards.

Appendix B 103

A. Fuller.

P.S. Bro^r Sutcliff is more than ordinarily concerned for Bro^r F. as his turn of mind previous to the meeting in Kett^g Vestry afforded a Serious objection to his going: and it is supposed the Society w^d not have consented to his going but for that Bro^r Sutcliff was for it, alledging that Bro^r F. having smarted already for his conduct at Oakham, he hoped he had learned wisdom by it, & there w^d be no danger.

A few hints to bro^r Carey &c.

1. The sense of many passages is prevented by the supplements <u>is</u> and <u>there are</u> in Ps. 16. 11. It means that God w^d raise him from the dead, wh. as he was the first who passed that way, from mortality to immortality, it was God who showed it him—and <u>thou wilt show me</u> is understood in each of the following sentences.

Hos.11.8. leave out the <u>how</u> in the second and fourth questions, and it will be an alternative appeal to his own compassion and to Ephraims conscience, wh. is ten times more forcible than one continued appeal to himself.

2. Some, (particularly Mr Zenas Trivet a bap^t min^r at Langham, who has raised among his connexions above 130£ tow^{ds} the Translation) thinks that the prophets, & the Epistles should be arranged according to the order of time in wh. they were written. I could send you, but not now, a Scheme of them, as also of the prophesies of Jeremiah, wh. are a bundle of papers put together without any respect to order.

3. Tho' I am neither a critic nor the son of a critic, yet I sometimes consult a little with Dr Common Sense, and he one day suggested that the account of <u>The body of Moses</u> in Jude 9 most certainly refer not to any tradition known among the jews, but to the story in Zech. 3. and I suppose if so, the word Μασεως (I think it is) was put there by the mistake of some transcriber for Ιεσους[5] or Joshua. So also Matt.27.9. must be either a mistake of a transcriber, putting Jeremy for Zachary; or the last chapters of Zechariah were not his, but written by Jeremiah. I cannot decide this question; but a learned friend of mine contends for the latter, and alleges that some of the things predicted in those chapters were fulfilled between the times of Jeremiah and Zechariah.

---

5. Transcriber's note: Both Greek words mentioned here are misspellings. The reader will do well to remember that these letters are personal correspondences—not necessarily intended to be published material.

A. F.
London. May 13. 99.

ANDREW FULLER TO WILLIAM CAREY: 6 AUGUST 1803

To Mr. Carey, Mission House, Serampore, Bengal.
Kett^g Aug. 6. 1803.
My dear brother Carey!

I have just finished a letter to you <u>all</u>; and now if I can I will say something to each of you. My years (now in my fiftieth) might be supposed to be accompanied with wisdom: but I know not any period of my religious life in wh. I have felt more of the justness of the complaint of Agur, "Surely I am more brutish than any man, and have not the understand^g of a man!" It is not to complain but I feel such a proneness to sink into supineness, and carelessness about everything, as is exceedingly discouraging to me. I was told yesterday of a clergyman who dreamed that a voice addressed him to this effect—You have received several hundreds a year for preaching, and what have you done? Is there one soul in your perish who has been turned to God by your preaching? His conscience answered, No; and waking from his sleep he presently died! I cannot but hope that many have been turned to God by mine; yet I am not without fears at times that I myself may at last be cast away! Such fears however are not habitual; but if I have any spirituality it is but as the smoking flax; now and then a groan and a desire after God. I am not ignorant that God has given me some talents, such as if I were more devoted to him might be much more useful than they are. Yet after all I must press forward; hoping to the end; tho' faint, yet pursuing. I found several passages to express the desires of my heart as I rode home f^m Olney yesterday. "Take not thy Holy Spirit from me! Forsake me not utterly! Wilt Thou not revive me? One of the young men at Olney (Bliss) was telling me his inward discouragements, and how he was ready to doubt the reality of his personal religion; and yet he had no desire to go back and relinquish the work of God. His feelings much accorded with mine. My dear bro^r! I have often read complaints of this sort in your letters; and I could as often have made similar complaints in return: but let us rather pray for each other, & strengthen each other's hands in the Lord. It is wonderful that God should do anything by such poor grovelling sinners as we are. One thing however is manifested by it, that the work is entirely his own; and if we should reach the kingdom of God at last, it will be by great grace. God has honoured us not a little by employing us in this great work: but as the honour does not belong to us, we must return it. The crowns do not seem to fit our heads; therefore they must be cast at the feet of Jesus. Such are the feelings of my heart.

We feel concerned about your health. You say in y^{rs} of Feb.2. You have had a Cold, and some spasmodic affections in your breast. We doubt not but you will use all possible means for the preservation of your health for the Lord's sake; tho' we are not without fear from your abounding labours.

The New Testament via America, and the Pentateuchs are arrived; as also a box of pieces. I have also rec^d a letter f^m Col. Bie, for wh will thank you to present my acknowledgements to him. I have remitted according to your desire, £21. 10. 0. to Mrs Short, and wh. we shall consider as we do every other of your orders as money remitted to the Missionaries. I find several letters from us to you & f^m you to us miscarry—We must not therefore think that either neglect the other when letters do not come. "My dear bro^r your domestic griefs are not forgotten by your friends. Grace be with you & y^{rs}

Y^r affect^{ts} bro^r
A. FULLER

P.S. Bro^r Ward in a letter to me some time ago expressed a wish that your son Felix sh^d come and be at Bristol a year or two for his improvement. Bro^r Ryland was mentioning it yesterday[6]

ANDREW FULLER TO WILLIAM CAREY: 10 JANUARY 1810

Dr Carey, Fort William College, Calcutta, Bengal.
Kett^g. Jan. 10th 1810.
My very dear bro^r Carey!

Yesterday I wrote you regretting that we had had no communications this season, & this morning 3 letters arrived, viz. y^{rs} of Mar. 27. 1809; one from Bro^r Ward <u>without</u> date, or signature, or conclusion, but which must have been written about the same time; and a journal f^m Jan.1. to Mar.8. of bro^r Chamberlain. I hope the parcel including the Orissa Testaments will include some Cir. L^{rs} of wh. we are sadly deficient. None for June, July & Decr 1808 and Jany 1809. One for Feb. 1809 was inclosed in bro^r Ward's letter of this day, and wh. is very good. I rejoice

---

6. Transcriber's note: The remaining text in this letter is obscured.

in all the goodness of the Lord tow^{ds} you at Calcutta, Coamalty &c. Bro^r Chamberlain speaks of a society (of soldiers, I suppose) at Berhampore. "The brethren of Serampore (he says) <u>do not advise to baptize them</u>." I was aware of the delicacy of his visiting those people when I first heard of it, on acc^t of its being the residence of Mr Parsons—yet it seems too much to neglect any part of the revealed will of Christ in complaisance to any man. I think were I there I sh^d first tell Mr Parsons himself, and afterwards then, that I did not wish to baptize any person <u>there</u>, but if any of them applied to me at Cutwa, I should not refuse it.

I have lately found some encouragement in my work. Having for more than a year past been more than heretofore been led to insist on the gospel way of salvation thro' a crucified Christ, I think I have of late seen some of the effects among the young people. During the past year we had a female member died. She had for the last 25 years been a useful good woman, but her husband was a perfect sot. I will tell you a few particulars of the family of this good woman. She by her industry nearly maintained her husband, & bro't up 4 children. She lived to see her daughter married, & her sons settled in business. Her eldest son has been baptized. Her second son a hopeful character. Her daughter's husband was about a year ago a wicked Antinomian; but God has met with him & he is become a little child. I baptized him lately. Soon after his baptism the mother died. Her poor old sot of a husband then remembered her counsels & prayers, and even he is become a new man. He weeps like a child, and wonders at himself. He never understood the gospel, he says, before tho' he has heard it many years. And now the married daughter weeps and says "I can see the change in my husband and in my father; but what am I?" The youngest son seeing his father weep, asks "What is the matter?" "O James!" replies the poor old man, "Come to Christ, come to Christ!" I preached a sermon to the youth last Lord's Day from 1 Thes.2.19. I think we must have had nearly 1000. They came from all quarters. My hearts desire and prayer for them is that they may be saved.

I find there is a new Baptist Academy begun in London. We have only heard that one of the late Mr Booth's deacons (Taylor of Newgate Street) has given a building for it with other accommodations, worth 3500£. I have a nephew at Bristol who goes on well, as I am told. I baptized him last summer. He has a strength of mind for learning rather extraordinary, and hardiness enough for a missionary.

Steadman goes on well in Yorkshire. Christopher Anderson who was a while with bro^r Sutcliff is doing good at Edinburgh. The Haldanes are paralyzed by Sandemanianism. I am now printing 12 letters agst that system. Poor Patterson & Henderson, who were sent out by them with a view of going to the East, but who stopped in Denmark and after that went to Sweden, are said to be deserted by them because they go not their lengths!

Mrs Timms (who was a Miss Rutt of Northampton) was taken off a week or two ago by a fever. Mrs Wallis who is now 72 years old, is ill of a fever at this time, but we hope not dangerous. She was pleased that you remembered her, and desires her kind love to you and all the missionaries. A lady lately died in Oxfordshire leaving 500£ to the Mission.

I have been obliged to use glasses for the last 7 years, but not of high magnifying powers. My upper teeth are mostly gone. I sit at the desk about 10 or 11 hours every day. I lately preached a sermon to the jews, and have written it out for printing. Have got pretty forward in a volume of sermons, three of which will be on justification. Have also a work in hand on the work of the ministry, in a series of letters to a friend: but I must finish the other first, or perhaps my course! I suppose there never was but one who before he died could say It is finished!

I have been used to understand the fruitful field being counted as a forest (in Isai. 32. 15) of the jewish church becoming a forest at what time the Gentile wilderness became a fruitful field. But I am now persuaded the meaning is, that when the spirit shall be poured out from on high not only shall the unevangelised parts of the world become a fruitful field, but those which have been most evangelised when compared with it shall be counted as a forest. A forest is something between a wilderness and a fruitful field. Some wood, some heath & now and then a cultivated spot—and answers to what the world has been hitherto as to religion in its most fruitful parts. "that which was wilderness, dry and barren, shall become a fruitful field; and that which we now reckon a fruitful field in comparison with what it shall be then, shall be counted for a forest." Henry.

I have sent Mrs Short the 5£ additional for you as desired.

Ever Y^{rs}
A. FULLER

Bibliography

Ahlstrom, Sidney E. *A Religious History of the American People.* New Haven: Yale University Press, 1972.

Ames, William. *The Marrow of Theology.* Translated by John D. Eusden. Boston: Pilgrim, 1968.

Anderson, Justice. "Medieval and Renaissance Missions (500-1792)." In *Missiology: An Introduction to the Foundations, History, and Strategies of World Missions,* edited by John Mark Terry, Ebbie Smith, Justice Anderson, 183-198. Nashville: Broadman & Holman, 1998

Beaver, R. Pierce. "The Genevan Mission to Brazil." In *The Heritage of John Calvin,* edited by John H. Bratt, 55-73. Grand Rapids: William B. Eerdmans, 1973.

Bebbington, D. W. *Evangelicalism in Modern Britain: A History from the 1730s to the 1980s.* London: Routledge, 1993.

Briggs, John. "The Influence of Calvinism on Seventeenth-Century English Baptists." *Baptist History and Heritage* 39, no. 2 (2004) 8-25.

Calhoun, David B. "John Calvin: Missionary Hero or Missionary Failure." *Presbyterian: Covenant Seminary Review* 5, no. 1 (1979) 16-33.

Calvin, John. *Calvin's Commentaries.* Vol. 1, *Commentaries on the First Book of Moses Called Genesis.* Translated by John King. Reprint, Grand Rapids: Baker, 2003.

———. *Calvin's Commentaries.* Vol. 4, *Commentary upon the Book of Psalms.* Translated by Arthur Golding. Reprint, Grand Rapids: Baker, 2003.

———. *Calvin's Commentaries.* Vol. 14, *The Commentaries of John Calvin on the Prophet Micah,* Translated by John Owen. Reprint, Grand Rapids: Baker, 2003.

———. *Calvin's Commentaries.* Vol. 17, *Commentary on a Harmony of the Evangelists, Matthew, Mark, and Luke.* Translated by William Pringle. Reprint, Grand Rapids: Baker, 2003.

———. *Calvin's Commentaries.* Vol. 19, *Commentaries on the Epistle of Paul the Apostle to the Romans,* Translated by John Owen. Reprint, Grand Rapids: Baker, 2003.

———. *Calvin's Commentaries.* Vol. 20, *Commentary on the Epistles of Paul the Apostle to the Corinthians.* Translated by John Pringle. Reprint, Grand Rapids: Baker, 2003.

———. "Calvin's Reply to Sadoleto." In *A Reformation Debate: John Calvin and Jacopo Sadoleto,* edited by John C. Olin, 49-94. Grand Rapids: Baker, 1966.

———. *Institutes of the Christian Religion.* Edited by John T. McNeill. Translated by Ford Lewis Battles. Library of Christian Classics, vols. 20-21. Philadelphia: Westminster, 1960.

———. *Letters of John Calvin.* Edited by Jules Bonnet. 4 vols. 1858; reprint, Eugene, OR: Wipf and Stock, 2007.

Chun, Chris. "A Mainspring of Missionary Thought: Andrew Fuller on Natural and Moral Inability." *American Baptist Quarterly* 25 (2006) 335-355.

Clipsham, Ernest F. "Andrew Fuller and the Baptist Mission." *Foundations* 10, no. 1 (1967) 4–18.

———. "Andrew Fuller and Fullerism: A Study in Evangelical Calvinism, 3. The Gospel Worthy of all Acceptation." *The Baptist Quarterly* 20, no. 5 (1964) 214–225.

———. "Andrew Fuller and Fullerism: A Study in Evangelical Calvinism, 4. Fuller as a Theologian." *Baptist Quarterly* 20, no. 6 (1964) 268–276.

Coates, Thomas. "Were the Reformers Mission-Minded." *Concordia Theological Monthly* 40 (1969) 600–611.

Davis, R. E. "The Great Commission from Calvin to Carey." *Evangel* 14 (1996) 44–49.

Dever, Mark. "The Doctrine of the Church." In *A Theology for the Church*, edited by Daniel L. Akin, 766–856. Nashville: B&H Academic, 2007.

Duesing, Jason G. "Counted Worthy: The Life and Thought of Henry Jessey, 1601–1663 Puritan Chaplain, Independent and Baptist Pastor, Millenarian Politician and Prophet." Ph.D. diss., Southwestern Baptist Theological Seminary, 2008.

———. "Luther Russell Bush III." *Southwestern Journal of Theology* 50, no. 1 (2007) 6–19.

Edwards, Jonathan. *The Works of Jonathan Edwards*. 2 vols. 1835; reprint, Peabody, MA: Hendrickson, 2000.

Erickson, Millard J. *Christian Theology*. Grand Rapids: Baker Academic, 1983.

Fuller, Andrew. *The Complete Works of Andrew Fuller*. Edited by Joseph Belcher. 3 vols. Harrisonburg, VA: Sprinkle, 1988.

———. The Letters of Andrew Fuller. (Typescript ms., gathered by Ernest A. Payne, Angus Library, Regents Park, Oxford University, Oxford).

Fuller, Richard. *Baptism and the Terms of Communion: An Argument*. Charleston, SC: Southern Baptist Publication Society, 1854.

Garrett, James Leo Jr. *Baptist Theology: A Four-Century Study*. Macon, GA: Mercer University Press, 2009.

———. *Systematic Theology: Biblical, Historical, and Evangelical*. 2 vols. Grand Rapids: William B. Eerdmans, 1995.

George, Timothy. "John Gill." In *Theologians in the Baptist Tradition*, edited by Timothy George, and David S. Dockery. Nashville: Broadman & Holman, 2001.

Gill, John. *A Body of Doctrinal and Practical Divinity*. Reprint, Paris, AR: The Baptist Standard Bearer, 1987.

Gonzalez, Justo L. *The Story of Christianity: The Early Church to the Present Day*. 2 vols. Peabody, MA: Prince Press, 2001.

Grantham, Thomas. "Dialogue between the Baptist and the Presbyterian." *Southwestern Journal of Theology* 48, no. 2 (2006) 189–214.

Greef, Wulfert de. *The Writings of John Calvin*. Translated by Lyle D. Bierma. Grand Rapids: Baker, 1993.

Grudem, Wayne. *Systematic Theology: An Introduction to Biblical Doctrine*. Grand Rapids: Zondervan, 1994.

Haykin, Michael A. G. "Andrew Fuller on Mission: Text and Passion." In *Baptists and Mission: Papers from the Fourth International Conference on Baptist Studies*. Studies in Baptist History and Thought, vol. 29, edited by Ian M. Randall, and Anthony R. Cross, 25–41. Colorado Springs: Paternoster, 2007.

———. "Hyper-Calvinism and the Theology of John Gill." Paper presented at the True Church Conference, Muscle Shoals, AL, 18–21 February 2010.

———. "John Calvin's Missionary Influence in France." *Reformation and Revival* 10, no. 4 (2001) 34–44.
Hughes, Philip E. "John Calvin: Director of Missions." In *The Heritage of John Calvin*, edited by John H. Bratt, 40–54. Grand Rapids: William B. Eerdmans, 1973.
Lane, Tony. *A Concise History of Christian Thought*. Grand Rapids: Baker, 2006.
Lindsay, Thomas M. *A History of the Reformation*. 2 vols. Edinburgh: T & T Clark, 1907.
Littell, Franklin H. "The Anabaptist Theology of Missions." *Mennonite Quarterly Review* 21, no. 1 (1947) 5–17.
———. *The Anabaptist View of the Church*. 1958; reprint, Paris, AR: The Baptist Standard Bearer, 2001.
———. "Protestantism and the Great Commission." *Southwestern Journal of Theology* 2, no. 1 (1959) 26–42.
Lumpkin, William L. *Baptist Confessions of Faith*. Valley Forge, PA: Judson, 1959.
Mauldin, A. Chadwick. "Transcriber's Preface to A Dialogue between the Baptist and the Presbyterian: An Early Baptist Responds to Calvinism." *Southwestern Journal of Theology* 48, no. 2 (2006) 183–188.
McBeth, Leon H. *The Baptist Heritage*. Nashville: Broadman, 1987.
McGrath, Alister E. *A Life of John Calvin: A Study in the Shaping of Western Culture*. Grand Rapids: Baker, 1990.
Morden, Peter. "Andrew Fuller as an Apologist for Missions." In *At the Pure Fountain of Thy Word: Andrew Fuller as an Apologist*. Studies in Baptist History and Thought, vol. 8, ed. Michael A. G. Haykin, 247–249. Waynesboro GA: Paternoster, 2004.
———. *Offering Christ to the World: Andrew Fuller and the Revival of Eighteenth-Century Particular Baptist Life*. Studies in Baptist History and Thought, vol. 8. Waynesboro, GA: Paternoster, 2003.
Morgan, Edmund S. *Visible Saints*. Ithaca, New York: Cornell University Press, 1963.
Muller, Richard A. "How Many Points." *Calvin Theological Journal* 28 (1993) 425–433.
Nelson, Stanley A. "Reflecting on Baptist Origins: The London Confession of Faith of 1644." *Baptist History and Heritage* 2, no. 29 (1994) 33–46.
Nettles, Tomas J. *Beginnings in Britain*. Vol. 1 of *The Baptists: Key People Involved in Forming a Baptist Identity*. Scotland: Christian Focus, 2005.
———. *By His Grace and for His Glory: A Historical, Theological, and Practical Study of the Doctrines of Grace in Baptist Life*. Lake Charles, LA: Cor Meum Tibi, 2002.
Newman, Albert Henry. *A Manual of Church History*. 2 vols. Philadelphia: The American Baptist Publication Society, 1902.
Oliver, Robert W. "Andrew Fuller and Abraham Booth." In *At the Pure Fountain of Thy Word: Andrew Fuller as an Apologist*. Studies in Baptist History and Thought, vol. 8, edited by Michael A. G. Haykin, 203–222. Waynesboro, GA: Paternoster, 2004.
Partee, Charles. *The Theology of John Calvin*. Louisville: Westminster John Knox, 2008.
Piper, John. *Desiring God: Meditations of a Christian Hedonist*. Sisters, OR: Multnomah, 1986.
———. "For Whom Did Jesus Taste Death?" No pages. Online: http://www.desiring god.org/ResourceLibrary/ Sermons/ByDate/1996/958_For_Whom_Did_Jesus_ Taste _Death.
———. *The Justification of God*. Grand Rapids: Baker Books, 1993.
———. "What Does Piper Mean When He Says He's a Seven Point Calvinist?" No pages. Online: http://www.desiringgod.org/ResourceLibrary/AskPastorJohn/By

Topic/105/1418_What_does_John_Piper_mean_when_he_says_that_he_is_a _sevenpoint_ Calvinist/.

Ramirez, Alonzo. "Missiological Perspectives of Calvin's Old Testament Interpretation: Implications for Theology of Mission." Paper presented at the Southeastern regional meeting of the Evangelical Theological Society, Dayton, TN, 7–8 March 1997.

Renihan, James H. "An Examination of the Possible Influence of Menno Simons' Foundation Book upon the Particular Baptist Confession of 1644." *American Baptist Quarterly* 15 (1996) 190–207.

———. "John Spilsbury." In *The British Particular Baptists: 1638–1910*, Vol. 1. Edited by Michael A. G. Haykin, 21–37. Springfield, MO: Particular Baptist, 1998.

Roberts, Phil. "Andrew Fuller." In *Theologians of the Baptist Tradition*, edited by Timothy George and David S. Dockery, 34–51. Nashville: Broadman & Holman, 2001.

Scott, Thomas, translator. *The Articles of the Synod of Dort*. Philadelphia: Presbyterian Board of Publication, 1856.

Simons, Menno. *The Complete Writings of Menno Simons*. Edited by John Christian Wenger. Translated by Leonard Verduin. Scottdale, PA: Herald, 1956.

Stanley, Brian. *The History of the Baptist Missionary Society, 1792–1992*. Edinburgh: T&T Clark, 1992.

Stassen, Glen. "Anabaptist Influence in the Origin of the Particular Baptists." *Mennonite Quarterly Review* 36 (1962) 322–48.

———. "Opening Menno Simons's Foundation-Book and Finding the Father of Baptist Origins Alongside the Mother-Calvinist Congregationalism." *Baptist History and Heritage* 33 (1998) 34–44.

Underwood, A. C. *A History of the English Baptists*. London: The Baptist Union of Great Britain and Ireland, 1947.

Verduin, Leonard. *The Reformers and Their Stepchildren*. Reprint, Paris, AR: The Baptist Standard Bearer, 1964.

Verkuyl, J. *Contemporary Missiology: An Introduction*. Translated by Dale Cooper. Grand Rapids: William B. Eerdmans, 1978.

Voolstra, Sjouke. "Menno Simons." In *The Reformation Theologians: An Introduction to Theology in the Early Modern Period*. Edited by Carter Lindberg, 363–77. Malden, MA: Blackwell, 2002.

Warneck, Gustav. *Outline of a History of Protestant Missions from the Reformation to the Present Time*. Edited by George Robson. New York: Fleming H. Revell, 1902.

Wenger, John Christian. Introd. to "The Foundation of Christian Doctrine." In *The Complete Writings of Menno Simons*, by Menno Simons. Scottdale, PA: Herald, 1956.

White, B. R. *The English Baptists of the Seventeenth Century*. Oxford: The Baptist Historical Society, 1996.

Wilson, Paul R. "William Kiffin." In *The British Particular Baptists: 1638–1910*, Vol. 1. Edited by Michael A. G. Haykin, 65–77. Springfield, MO: Particular Baptist, 1998.

Wright, Stephen. *The Early English Baptists, 1603–1649*. Rochester, NY: The Boydell, 2006.

Yarnell, Malcolm B., III. *The Formation of Christian Doctrine*. Nashville: B&H Academic, 2007.

———. "The Heart of a Baptist." *Criswell Theological Review* 4, no. 1 (2006) 73–87.

Young, Doyle L. "Andrew Fuller and the Modern Mission Movement." *Baptist History and Heritage* 17, no. 4 (1982) 17–27.

Subject/Name Index

A

Ames, William, 23, 26
amillennialism, 2
Anabaptist, 10, 19, 20, 21, 43, 44, 45, 46, 63–64, 68
antinomianism, 66
apostolic succession, 17, 41, 43, 68
Arminian, 13
Arminianism, 66
Augustine, 47

B

Baptist Missionary Society, 28, 49, 50–55, 60, 65
Barebone, Praise God, 22, 23
Barrow, William, 53
Batte, Timothy, 16, 22
Batten, Jan, 16
believers's baptism, 25
Bellius, Martin, 47
Beza, Theodore, 47
biblical authority, 9
Blunt, Richard, 16, 22
BMS. *See* Baptist Missionary Society
Booth, Abraham, 56
Brainerd, David, 28
Briggs, John, 23, 25
Bunyan, John, 5, 19
Bush, L.R., 5

C

Calhoun, David, 35, 37, 39, 40, 43, 44
Calvin, John, 10, 12, 23, 24, 28, 29, 30–32, 33, 34–40, 41–48, 66, 67, 68, 69, 70, 71

Calvinism, 1–2, 3–4, 5–7, 9, 10, 11, 12, 13, 14, 15, 17, 19, 23, 25, 27–28, 29, 35, 48, 56, 60, 65, 66, 67, 70, 71
Calvinistic. *See* Calvinism
Carey, William, 28, 43, 50, 51, 52, 53, 54, 55, 63, 70
Castellio, Sebastian, 47
Charles IX, 40
Clipsham, Ernest, 50, 51, 53, 54, 60, 62, 63, 65
Coates, Thomas, 43
Collegiants, 16
compatibilism, 4

D

Dagg, J. L., 5, 6
Davis, R. E., 43
Dever, Mark, 2, 11
Divine decrees, 56
doctrines of grace, 5
Donatism, 45
dortian Calvinism, 3, 5, 7, 12, 13, 23
double predestination, 7
Duesing, Jason, 5, 15, 16

E

East India Company, 53, 54
easy believism, 7
Eaton, Samuel, 15
ecclesiology, 1, 12, 13, 31, 34, 67
Edwards, Jonathan, 7, 8, 28
Edwardsian, 12, 59
election, 3, 5, 8, 23, 24, 56
eschatological, 62, 68, 69

eternal justification, 10
eternal security. *See* perseverance of the saints
evangelical Calvinism, 28
evangelicalism, 9, 71

F

Farel, William, 31, 46
Featley, Daniel, 18
five point Calvinism, 1
foreknowledge, 3
Francis I, 30, 37
Fuller, Andrew, 5, 6, 7, 9, 10, 11–12, 13, 14, 27–28, 49, 50–54, 55–59, 60–65, 66, 67, 68, 69, 70, 71
Fuller, Richard, 11
Fullerism, 11, 60, 65, 66, 67, 70, 71

G

Garrett, James Leo, 3, 5, 7, 9, 12, 14, 24, 28
General Baptists, 13
George, Timothy, 2, 10
Gill, John, 5, 10
Grant, Charles, 53
Grantham, Thomas, 13, 14, 47, 48
Great Commission, 9–10, 33, 34, 41–44, 59, 61, 63–65, 68, 69, 70, 71
Grigg, Jacob, 50
Grudem, Wayne, 3–4

H

Haykin, Michael A.G., 2, 10, 35, 37, 38, 63
Hubmaier, Balthasar, 10
Hughes, Philip, 39, 40
hyper-Calvinism, 10, 27, 28, 56, 60, 65

I

immersion, 16, 18, 19, 21, 22, 25
inerrancy, 5
irresistible grace, 1, 4, 6, 8

J

Jacob, Henry, 15, 50
Jessey, Henry, 15
JLJ church, 15–16, 18
justification, 10, 24, 37, 46

K

Keach, Benjamin, 5
Kiffin, William, 18–19
Knox, John, 39

L

Lamb, Thomas, 16
Lathrop, John, 15, 18
limited atonement, 1, 4, 6, 14
Lindsay, Thomas, 39
Littell, Franklin, 41, 63, 64
London Confession, 13, 14, 15, 16, 18, 19–26
Luther, Martin, 5, 20, 32, 33

M

magisterial reform, 40, 41, 44, 45, 48, 70, 71
Magisterial Reformer, 68
Matthew 28. *See* Great Commission
McBeth, Leon, 13, 15, 16, 19
Melanchthon, Philipp, 33
missiology, 1, 12, 13, 28, 29, 32, 35, 41, 48, 49, 65, 66, 67, 69
missionary, 10, 12, 28, 29, 31, 32, 33, 34, 35, 36, 38, 40, 49, 50–55, 60, 61, 62, 63, 64, 65, 67, 68, 69, 70, 71
Mohler, Al, 2
moral depravity, 59
moral inability, 59
Morden, Peter J., 27, 49, 52, 53, 60, 62, 71
Muller, Richard A., 1, 2, 9, 25
Mullins, E. Y., 5, 6
Münster revolution, 20

N

natural ability, 59
Nelson, Stanley, 14, 23
neo-Donatists, 45
Nettles, Thomas, 5–7, 10, 17, 18
New Light Calvinism, 12

O

original sin, 46

P

paedobaptism, 11, 17, 20, 25, 46
Partee, Charles, 24, 31, 38
Particular Baptists, 10, 13, 14–16, 17, 18, 19, 20, 21, 22, 23–26, 27, 67
perseverance of the saints, 1, 4, 7, 8
personal conversion, 9, 48
Piper, John, 7–9
post-Constantinian, 45
predestination, 17, 37
preparation. *See* preparationism
preparationism, 26, 58
preterition, 24
Protestant Reformation, 25, 34
Protestant Reformers, 29, 32, 45

R

Ramirez, Alonzo, 34, 35
Reformed, 1, 2, 4, 7, 9, 11, 12, 13, 14, 23, 24, 25, 26, 27, 63, 67
regenerate church, 9, 10, 11
Remonstrant controversy, 1
Renihan, James, 17, 22
reprobation, 3, 7, 23, 24

S

sanctification, 24, 31, 37
Servetus, Michael, 45–47, 68, 70
Simons, Menno, 19–22, 64, 67
Smyth, John, 13

sola scriptura, 25, 26
soteriology, 1, 2, 4, 5, 6, 12, 13, 14, 15, 23, 29, 67
sovereignty, 4, 8, 38, 61
Spilsbury, John, 16–17
Stassen Glen, 20–22
Synod of Dort, 24, 26

T

total depravity, 1, 3, 6, 8, 24
Trinity, 46
True Confession, 21, 23
Twining, Richard, 53
two swords, 45

U

unconditional election, 1, 3, 5, 6, 23, 24
Underwood, A. C., 15, 16

V

Velore uprising, 53
Verduin, Leonard, 45, 47
Verkuyl, J., 32

W

Waring, John Scott, 53
Warneck, Gustav, 32–35
warrant of faith, 27, 32, 56, 59
Wilberforce, William, 53, 54
Wright, Stephen, 13, 16, 22

Y

Yarnell, Malcolm, 9, 10, 26, 43
Young, Doyle, 10, 28, 50, 51, 52, 54

Z

Zwingli, Ulrich, 32

www.ingramcontent.com/pod-product-compliance
Lightning Source LLC
Chambersburg PA
CBHW050846160426
43192CB00011B/2166